CROSS-NATIONAL RESEARCH
METHODOLOGY & PRACTICE

Cross-National Research Methodology & Practice offers practical guidance for relative newcomers to cross-national comparative research by analysing and evaluating the research process, focusing strongly on best practice in terms of methods and management. It raises a number of important issues for cross-national researchers which have been given insufficient attention in discussions of methods and practice.

The volume contains reflexive and theoretically based pieces on the development of contextualization as an approach to cross-national comparative research, using qualitative and quantitative methods, extending to the integration of different methodological approaches.

Practical examples are drawn from cross-national research projects to illustrate different methods ranging from:

- biographical and documentary approaches;
- the collection and analysis of socio-demographic and attitudinal survey data either carried out by lone researchers or teams of researchers;
- the exploration of internet sources and application of computer analysis to quantitative and qualitative data.

The collection provides a firm focus on methodological issues relating to context, values and discourse.

This book was previously published as a special issue of *Social Research Methodology: Theory & Practice*.

Linda Hantrais is Professor of European Social Policy at Loughborough University and Visiting Fellow at the Centre for International Studies, London School of Economics.

Steen Mangen is Senior Lecturer in the Department of Social Policy at the London School of Economics.

CROSS-NATIONAL RESEARCH METHODOLOGY & PRACTICE

Linda Hantrais & Steen Mangen

Routledge
Taylor & Francis Group

LONDON AND NEW YORK

First published 2007 by Routledge
2 Park Square, Milton Park, Abingdon, Oxon OX14 4RN

Routledge is an imprint of the Taylor & Francis Group, an informa business

Transferred to Digital Printing 2009

© 2007 Linda Hantrais & Steen Mangen

British Library Cataloguing in Publication Data
A catalogue record for this book is available from the British Library

ISBN10: 0–415–41140–8 (hbk)
ISBN10: 0–415–49459–1 (pbk)

ISBN13: 978–0–415–41140–0 (hbk)
ISBN13: 978–0–415–49459–5 (pbk)

CONTENTS

Published in association with the Social Research Association (SRA). The Social Research Association is open to all those interested or involved in social research. Its main purpose is to advance the conduct, development and use of social research across all sectors.

Preface

Cross-National Research

LINDA HANTRAIS and STEEN MANGEN

Discussion about cross-national social research methods has centred on at least three fundamental considerations. A long-standing debate has revolved around the question of whether cross-national social research constitutes a legitimated set of methods in its own right, or is merely a manifestation of more general issues arising in the field. Genericists have insisted that, despite specific constraints in operationalizing methods in international settings, there are no distinct cross-national methods per se. Others advance the argument that paramount problems to do with language, space and culture are sufficient to justify particularism as a research entity.

A second facet relates to the competing objectives of cross-national investigation. Much of the officially sponsored policy research is primarily dictated by pressures to extract 'lessons from the homeland'. Only in more recent times has a more robust scientific agenda been established with attempts to construct reasonably well-defined models and, in limited cases, to test theory. Often, effort has been handicapped by methodology which restricts samples to very narrow 'most similar' countries, and which imposes too brief a time scale to disentangle the social, cultural, economic and political variables. To these must be added the tendency in quantitative comparative research for over-reliance on highly-aggregated data, which exposes the researcher to the dangers of a large degree of multicolinearity.

Finally, frustrations are ever present in reaching effective management of projects, leading to the colonialization of methods, dominance of research approaches and, leadership by particular academic and national traditions.

For these reasons, much of the literature on the cross-national comparative research process tends to give precedence to thematic content and findings rather than focusing on the theory and practice of the research. The growing interest in cross-national comparisons within the social sciences since the 1970s has not, therefore, been matched by commensurate advances at the theoretical and practical level. As a result, the material collected in international projects is often not directly comparable, and the findings reported to sponsors may be biased or misleading.

The aim of *Cross-National Research Methodology & Practice* is to contribute to the theoretical basis of research that crosses national boundaries and to offer practical guidance for relative newcomers to cross-national research by analysing and evaluating the research process. The contributions include reflexive and theoretically-based pieces on the development of contextualization as an approach to cross-national comparative research, on qualitative and quantitative methods, extending to the integration of different methodological approaches. Shorter articles exemplify the practice of carrying out cross-national comparisons, focusing again on analysis of the research process. All the papers provide practical examples from cross-national research projects, illustrating different methods which range from biographical and documentary approaches, the collection and analysis of socio-demographic and attitudinal survey data, whether carried out by lone researchers or teams, the exploration of internet sources, and application of computer analysis to quantitative and qualitative data. A theme common to three of the shorter papers is the study of migration. They raise a number of important issues for cross-national research that have not, hitherto, been given sufficient attention in discussions of methods and practice.

Contextualization in cross-national comparative research

LINDA HANTRAIS

Introduction

The many definitions of cross-national comparative research in the social sciences have in common their concern to observe social phenomena across nations, to develop robust explanations of similarities or differences, and to attempt to assess their consequences, whether it be for the purposes of testing theories, drawing lessons about best practice or, more straightforwardly, gaining a better understanding of how social processes operate. Much of the comparative research undertaken in the early postwar period, particularly the large-scale studies carried out by political scientists in the USA, aimed to produce generalizations from the US experience, assuming them to be universally applicable. At the other extreme, proponents of culturalist explanation upheld that social reality could only be properly understood within the context in which it occurs, and that all findings are conditioned by spatial and temporal factors, and are not, therefore, amenable to generalization. In attempting to reconcile these two conflicting approaches, another body of cross-national comparative research has

Linda Hantrais holds a chair in the Department of European Studies and is Director of its European Research Centre, at Loughborough University, Leicestershire LE11 3TU, UK; e-mail: L.Hantrais@lboro.ac.uk She is convenor of the Cross-National Research Group. Her recent publications include (edited with Steen Mangen) *Cross-National Research Methods in the Social Sciences* (Pinter, 1996) and (edited) *Gendered Policies in Europe: Reconciling Employment and Family Life* (Macmillan, 2000).

sought to identify general factors within social systems that can be interpreted with reference to specific societal contexts.

Contextualization is central to all three of these approaches. In the first case, social reality is considered to be context free; in the second, it is context bound, and the context is an object of study in its own right; in the third, social reality is also context dependent, but the context itself serves as an important explanatory variable and an enabling tool, rather than constituting a barrier to effective cross-national comparisons.

This paper explores the growing interest among social scientists in issues surrounding contextualization as a major component in cross-national comparative studies. It argues that an in-depth understanding of the socio-cultural, economic and political contexts in which social phenomena develop is a precondition for successful cross-national comparative research. It addresses a number of methodological questions, arising in research that crosses national boundaries. Firstly, how to justify adopting the nation as the contextual framework; how to select and delimit contextual factors; how to identify the most appropriate research paradigms; how to take account of culturally determined research conventions; how to deal with conceptual equivalence in different cultural and linguistic settings; and how to integrate contextual factors when interpreting and evaluating findings. Reference is made to examples from multinational and interdisciplinary projects, using both quantitative and qualitative methods, to illustrate how these issues have been tackled and resolved, and to identify best practice.

From context-free to context-bounded research

The comparative method has a long pedigree in the social sciences. It was used by the founders of modern sociology, Auguste Comte and Herbert Spencer, to establish models of social evolution. John Stuart Mill provided an early systematized account of the comparative method, which was subsequently adopted by Max Weber and Emile Durkheim in their observations of industrial capitalism, the division of labour, religion and other social processes.

Universalist approaches

The search for constant factors or general laws capable of explaining social phenomena, as advocated by the early sociologists, underpinned much of the international comparative research undertaken in the 1950s and 1960s. It was grounded in the assumption that universal characteristics could be identified in social phenomena, independently from a specific context. For Dogan and Pelassy (1990: 19), in comparative politics, 'the very spirit of comparison involves the quest for universals'. This is because universalist theory was culture or context free, 'landless' theory according to Rose (1991: 446), also with reference to political science. It followed that generalizations could be made from the observation of social processes in a given society, culture or nation. One of the conclusions drawn on the basis of this type of research was that industrial societies would undergo the same evolutionary process and ultimately converge (Wilensky and Lebeaux 1958). The notion of culture-free contexts was applied in the study of organizations in the 1970s to argue for a scientifically determined 'one best way' in organizational management, as critiqued by Rose (1985). In the field of social policy, attempts in the 1980s and 1990s to explain the crisis of welfare (Mishra 1984), to classify welfare states (Esping-Andersen 1990) and to predict the future of welfare in the context of economic integration and globalization (Esping-Andersen 1996) were part of the search for normative models from which generalizations could be made. The universalist approach has also served as a basic tenet in many econometric studies aimed at modelling behaviour, at times with seemingly little regard for social reality (Allsopp 1995).

The universalist approach to cross-national comparison, with its emphasis on the search for similarity and convergence, often as a means of testing the wider applicability of a theory developed at national level, can thus be criticized for ignoring specific contexts and for treating cultural factors as exogenous variables. Studies based on universalist theory have also been reproached for drawing what may be ill-founded inferences about causality at individual level by deduction or extrapolation from relationships established between variables at aggregate level. Indeed, researchers may fall into the trap of 'ecological' or 'wrong level fallacy', identified by US sociologists many decades ago (Robinson 1951, Riley 1963), whereby the wrong conclusions about causality are drawn because the wrong level of inference is being used.

Culturalist approaches

While large-scale comparative research was engaged in tracking and mapping the development of socio-political and economic phenomena across the world, a very different approach was being pursued in another body of research, with the focus on national uniqueness and particularism, and cross-cultural contrasts or differences. For proponents of culture-boundedness or relativism, contextualization was at the nexus of comparative research, and the existence of truly universal concepts and values was rejected. Culturalism, as developed initially by the Chicago School from observation of cultural diversity in the urban environment in the 1920s and 1930s, placed such great emphasis on social contexts and their specificity, distinctiveness or uniqueness, that meaningful comparisons and generalizations were made very difficult, if not impossible. Culturalism drew heavily on ethnographic accounts to illustrate diversity and divergence rather than similarity and convergence. Taken to the extreme by ethnomethodologists, such as Garfinkel in the 1960s, social reality was seen as a 'rational accomplishment' of individuals. Claims that generalizations could be made on the basis of individual accounts have not received much credence in the sociological literature, and the potential for transporting concepts and values identified as being peculiar to a particular society into another cultural or linguistic community would seem to be limited.

Societal approaches

To overcome the obstacles to effective comparative research associated with universalism and culturalism, many intermediate positions have been adopted. In the 1960s, the neo-evolutionists, among them Parsons, developed a theory that took account of the efficiency of different societies in adapting to evolutionary advances. Such an approach allowed limited comparisons to be made of subsets of societies at different stages in the process of development. In their search for a compromise position, Przeworski and Teune (1970: 12) expressed the view that general theories can be formulated if it is recognized that 'social phenomena are not only diverse but always occur in mutually interdependent and interacting structures, possessing a spatiotemporal location. If stable, these patterns of interaction can be treated as systems'. By treating social phenomena as components of systems, it follows that explanations of behaviour must be examined with reference to factors intrinsic to the system in question. The two authors argue, however, that the conclusion should not be drawn that systems are unique; part of the explanation for social reality may be found in factors extrinsic to the system, enabling more general or universal factors to be identified.

In moving away from the universalist approach in the study of organizations, Lammers and Hickson (1979: 403) identified three ways in which an organization could be affected (or culturally bound) by the cultural patterns prevailing in its social environment. Firstly, political and legal agencies prescribe and proscribe certain procedures and provisions, which in turn affect the values espoused by the organization, its suppliers and customers. Secondly, dominant elites within the organization design and redesign its structure in line with culturally-embedded norms and practices. Thirdly, members of organizations import values, norms and roles from external subcultures, such as family, education, community, peer group, influencing how they organize internally. In demonstrating how organizations are culture bound, the analysis was intended to identify and explain distinctiveness by investigating the interplay between organizations and their societal settings. Comparative research into industrial relations, and more especially trade unions, has also recognized the value of analysing nationally-specific institutional frameworks as generators of norms, practices and mutual expectations, but with the proviso that trade union movements are so culturally specific that they are, essentially, 'non-comparable' (Hyman 1998: 57).

Maurice (1989) of the Aix group is generally attributed with having further articulated and applied what has come to be known as the 'societal' approach in the study of organizations. From the late 1960s, he and his colleagues were also trying to steer a course between the extremes of universalism and culturalism. They argued that all international comparisons aim to demonstrate the effect of the national context on the object of study, but with the purpose of determining the extent to which generalizations can be made from the theoretical models and hypotheses that the researcher is seeking to test empirically. Therefore, they rejected any form of analysis which directly compared 'equivalent' terms (like with like). Instead, stress was laid on the importance of analysing the relationship between the macro and the micro, implying an interaction between a plurality of causal factors, on the grounds that actors cannot be separated from structures and *vice versa*, since they are all socially constructed. According to this line of argument, comparisons are made possible by the fact that each unit of observation has a systemic coherence and is part of a process, rooted in national specificity. It follows that the globalization of technology does not, for example, eliminate the diversity of social forms, but nor does it prevent generalizations.

The conclusion to be drawn from this analysis of the main approaches adopted in cross-national comparisons is that researchers embarking on comparative studies would be well advised to avoid the extremes of universalism and culturalism. If their aim is to observe social phenomena across nations, develop robust explanations of similarities or differences, and attempt to assess the consequences, they could usefully combine the strong points contained in the different approaches outlined above. As shown by the examples quoted of the societal approach, the compromise it implies does not represent an easy solution, and none of the studies mentioned offers a blueprint that can be readily applied in all cross-national research.

The nation as the contextual frame of reference

In differentiating between universalist, culture-bound and societal approaches, Grootings (1986) has distinguished between 'cross-national research' and what he terms 'international comparative research'. He categorized cross-national (universalist and culturalist) comparative research as descriptive and deductive whereas international (societal) comparative research, as espoused by Maurice and others, was seen as establishing a relationship between the macro and micro levels, involving a more analytical and deductive approach. This terminological distinction has not been widely followed in the English-language literature, where the prefix 'cross' is used ubiquitously to describe studies that are cross-cultural, cross-country, cross-systemic, cross-institutional, cross-societal, or even cross-disciplinary (Øyen 1990).[1] Rather than focusing on the implications of adopting the prefix 'cross' or 'inter', it could be argued that the more important question is whether 'nation' is the most appropriate unit of analysis, or frame of reference, for studies such as those described in the present volume and the social sciences in general.[2]

The rationale for selecting nation states as a unit of analysis or frame of reference for comparative research is relatively easy to justify in studies where the criterion for inclusion is their membership of an international organization, such as the European Union (EU), the Council of Europe, the Organization for Economic Cooperation and Development (OECD), the

International Labour Organization (ILO) or the Commonwealth of Independent States (CIS). In the case of the EU, for example, national governments are directly represented on the EU's supreme decision-making body, the Council of Ministers, and through nationally elected members of the European Parliament. Even in federal states, such as Germany, it is central, rather than regional or local, government that is represented in Brussels.

Nations, or nation states, afford a convenient frame of reference for comparative studies since they possesss clearly defined territorial borders, and their own characteristic administrative and legal structures. 'Nation' is, however, a contested and loaded concept. National borders shift and, it cannot be assumed that they necessarily correspond to cultural, linguistic and ethnic divisions, or to a common sense of identity. German unification, for example, created a national unit in which internal diversity was greater in some respects (socio-demographic trends) than that observed across the EU. Teune (1990) prefers the term 'country' on the grounds that it is more readily 'specifiable', but 'cross-country' has semantic connotations in English that researchers may want to avoid. Many authors use country and nation interchangeably, avoiding reference to 'cross-country' comparisons. Rose (1991), for example, argues that comparative analysis in political science excludes 'within-nation' comparison, but must focus on concepts that are applicable in more than one 'country'.

The adoption of the nation as the contextual unit may be complicated for reasons other than semantics. Firstly, just as national territorial boundaries shift, membership of international organizations undergoes change. In the case of the EU, the four waves of EU membership between the 1950s and 1990s altered not only the size but also the socio-cultural structure of the community/union. The addition of new member states from Central and Eastern Europe in the twenty-first century is expected to bring further changes to the shape of social Europe. Secondly, again exemplified by the EU, a multilevel system of governance may operate, which means that individual member states are contributing to the formation of policy within international institutions while, at the same time, being obliged to ensure compliance at national level through their own legislation and institutions. Thirdly, a further complication in taking the nation as the context for comparative policy analysis arises from the way the policy formation process operates both at national and supranational level. Non-governmental organizations, issue networks, policy communities and interest groups are playing an increasingly important role as policy actors co-operating across national boundaries.

An objection often raised to studies that take the nation as the unit of observation is that within-nation differences may be obscured. In their work, Maurice (1989) and his colleagues analysed in great depth the national training and qualifications systems in three Western industrialized nations (France, Germany and the UK). Applying the same approach, Jobert (1996) soon discovered its limitations when she and her team attempted to extend work done in France on education, training and employment to Germany, Italy and the UK, because the focus on national systems obscured internal diversity. Dogan and Pelassy (1990: 18) talk of 'eight Spains ... three Belgiums, four Italys, and five or six Frances'. Analysis of the phenomenon of population ageing at national level, to take another example, conceals the fact that differences may be greater between the north and south of Italy, between former East and West Germany, or between the Paris region and the Limousin in France, than between individual EU member states (Hantrais 1999b).

The advantage for the comparative researcher of examining a particular social phenomenon using nations as the contextual framework when they are members of an international organization is that they explicitly share a common reference point. Belonging to the organization confers on them a certain identity of purpose through the common goals to which they subscribe as a condition of membership. At the same time, they exhibit cultural and social diversity at national and subnational level, due to the specific ways in which their legal, political, economic and socio-cultural systems have developed and operate. They, therefore, provide appropriate material for a multilevel analysis, capable of sustaining the diverse interests of universalists, culturalists and societalists, by affording an abundance of data on which to base observation, explanation and evaluation of the social situation.

Delimiting contexts

Few, if any, comparative studies set out to compare whole societies or to be comprehensive in their coverage of social systems. If a cross-national comparative study is to remain both tractable and credible, a major task for researchers engaged in studies that cross national boundaries is, therefore, how to select the most appropriate national and societal contexts for analysis without lapsing into the excesses of universalism or culturalism. In political science comparisons, Rose (1991: 447) has proposed adopting what he calls 'bounded variability', on the grounds that differences between countries have limits, as illustrated by the observation that the variations in the methods for electing a parliament are not infinite. The implication is that the researcher must determine how many units of analysis need to be included to ensure a balance between the number of different national cases considered necessary for representativeness and for optimal coverage of variability. Two-nation studies will not enable the researcher to conclude that one or other of them presents an aberrant case but it may not be necessary to examine a particular phenomenon in 150 different nations to identify the range of possible configurations. The two-nation study will, however, enable the researcher to investigate a much larger number of contextual or micro variables than is feasible in large-scale multinational studies.

For practical reasons, using a random sample may not be an option when determining the mix of countries to be studied, although the development of more sophisticated international socio-economic indicators and statistical datasets is making sampling a more feasible and reliable procedure. A form of stratified sampling can be said to operate when countries are selected according to such groupings based on the stage of economic development or demographic transition, or their membership of an international organization. Studies carried out across the member states belonging to large international organizations, such as the OECD (Eardley 1996), ILO (Lim 1996) or Council of Europe (Corden and Duffy 1998), can be considered as representative of a wider universe, or at least a significant part of it. While their representativeness will, by definition, be very limited, small-scale case studies can be situated in relation to a wider frame of reference, allowing for some extrapolation. Schunk's (1996) analysis of care options for older people was limited to only two cities, one in Germany (Nürnberg) and the other in the UK (Manchester), but she established a basis for comparison by situating them in relation to their national contexts. By constructing model cases and identifying pathways of health and social care, she was able to demonstrate how the individual transforms welfare resources into welfare outcomes, and how the experience of a particular welfare system can be located in relation to broader cultural settings and social structures.

Another approach to the selection of national cases depends on whether the researcher is more interested in analysing similarities or differences. In the 1970s, in the context of the debate about the relative merits of universalism *versus* culturalism, the question was extensively discussed as to whether research designs should be based on 'most similar' or 'most different' cases (in line with J.S. Mills' method of agreement or difference). Clearly, if a group of countries is selected because they have reached a similar stage of economic, political or social development, as illustrated by the extent of deregulation, pluralism or social inclusion, the interest of the comparison might lie in understanding the process whereby this situation was achieved, and in deciding whether any lessons can be drawn by less advanced nations from the experience recorded. If countries are selected according to the extent to which they differ from one another with reference to a particular phenomenon, the aim might be to establish how the differences can be explained and whether any common causal factors can be identified despite the diversity at national level.

More often than not the choice of comparators is determined by pragmatic factors and is justified *post hoc*. The sponsors of the research may have their own political reasons for insisting on the inclusion of certain countries: for example the need to involve poorer countries or nations with non-democratic regimes. The lone researcher will be constrained by financial and personal resources, not least knowledge of the relevant languages and cultures, and access to information. The larger research team will also be limited by internal and external constraints, including the composition of the team itself, as illustrated below. The country mix in studies of the whole of the EU is determined by the different waves of membership, each new group of countries adding new variants to an already heterogeneous group of nations and bringing different sets of interests that impact on the European policy agenda (Hantrais 1999a, 2000). The 'choice' of team members and the countries to be incorporated in the comparison is, however, critical in determining not only how the research process unfolds, which is too rarely an object of study in its own right (Hantrais and Mangen 1996), but also the findings. Any similarities or differences revealed by a cross-national study may be no more than an artifact of the choice of countries. At the very least, the researcher engaging in comparative studies should be able to present a scientific rationale for the mix of countries or nations selected and should report on the implications for the research method of the 'enforced' choice at the research design stage as well as in the interpretation of the findings.

It is desirable for researchers undertaking comparative studies to have an intimate knowledge of more than one society, their languages and cultures, and this would seem to be almost a prerequisite for embarking on scientifically grounded cross-national research projects adopting the societal approach. Even when the members of a research team possess an in-depth understanding of a number of societies, they still need to select the most appropriate contexts for analysis within those societies in relation to the social phenomena under investigation. The broader the country coverage, the greater the likelihood is that only a small number of within-country contexts can be examined. The smaller the number of countries included, in 'narrow-gauge' studies, according to Rose (1991: 455), the greater the contextual detail and the chances of approaching a more holistic comparison, and the easier it is to be consistent in specifying and applying concepts and in using qualitative evidence. The close-up (particularistic), medium (societal) and the long-distance (universal) views can, we suggest, all be justified but it has to be accepted that they will each reveal different social realities. Whatever the approach, the contextual factors to be examined are likely to be determined, in the first instance, by the topic of the research, the disciplinary perspective(s) inherent in the research design and the financial, temporal and human resources available. It is relatively rare for funding to be open-ended, and most research proposals have to be tailored to fit the resources on offer.

The possible contexts for analysis within nations are numerous. The following interdisciplinary checklist, though not comprehensive, indicates the most frequently examined contexts in cross-national comparative studies and over time:

- **Political institutions** – ideology, political systems, political parties, representation and power, pressure and interest groups, policy networks.
- **Administrative structures** – machinery of central, regional, local government, taxation, social security, labour administration, public, private organizations.
- **Economic systems** – financial institutions, economic sectors, firms, labour markets, trade, fiscal and employment policy, trade unions, globalization.
- **The legal framework** – national and supranational legislation, social security and labour law, implementation and good practice.
- **Social institutions and structures** – family, household, kinship, education and training (qualifications, skills), social stratification.
- **Social protection systems** – funding and benefit structures (housing, health, unemployment, old age, family, social assistance), social services, welfare delivery.

- **The cultural environment** – values, beliefs, elite structures, media, religion, leisure.
- **The physical environment** – ecology, pollution, climate.
- **Information technology** – industry, communications, employment, location.
- **Socio-demographic variables** – gender, ethnicity, age, generation, socio-occupational groups.

Since one of the justifications for selecting the nation state as the frame of reference is that it has an identifiable administrative and legal system, a valuable starting point is often to situate the social phenomenon under study with reference to its institutional settings. Without knowledge of the political regime or of legislation in a particular field, it may be difficult to grasp why it is, or is not, appropriate to investigate a particular topic. An analysis of industrial relations might involve an understanding of political institutions, social protection and educational and training systems, as well as employment policy (Hyman 1998). Families can usefully be defined in terms of national administrative and legal frameworks (Hantrais and Letablier 1996), and welfare states may best be understood by reference to the political economy in the countries under observation (Jones Finer 1999) or the impact of globalization (Esping-Andersen 1996).

In a study, for the ILO, of equal opportunities in employment as mediated by labour administration in China, Chile, France, Ghana and Romania (a selection of countries determined by political rather than scientific criteria), information was sought from national experts about the political regime, the degree of urbanization and economic development, national labour and social security law and benefits systems, employment trends, education and training provision, and literacy, before attempts anything approaching a comparative analysis of equal opportunities between women and men (Hantrais and Sineau 1998). A study of the interactive relationship between socio-demographic trends, social and economic policies within the EU involved collecting and analysing data on population decline and ageing, family formation and dissolution, gender and intergenerational relations, economic sectors, labour markets, economic development and monetary union, social spending, party politics and ideology, European social policy, national social protection systems and social legislation, as well as public debates (Byrne 1999, Hantrais 1999a, Hantrais 1999b, Hantrais and Lohkamp-Himmighofen 1999). The socio-economic tasks identified within the key action 'Improving the Socio-Economic Knowledge Base' under the European Commission's Framework Programme 5, launched in 1999, stressed the multidimensional nature of the socio-economic issues facing the Union, requiring researchers to take account of the overall European context, including European social and economic development models, enlargement, monetary union and the European situation in the world context. It also identified gender as a 'cross-cutting dimension', in line with the agreement reached at European level to mainstream gender.

The researcher's cultural context

From the perspective of the historian and with reference to immigration studies, Green (1994: 6) has argued that 'no comparison is completely neutral. By the level of generalization chosen, the variables chosen, the method of agreement or difference used, the accent is placed on diversity or unity. The way in which the question is asked implies part of the response.' This article shows how 'choices' of units and levels of analysis, and variables in cross-national comparisons are generally constrained, if not imposed, by external factors. It also suggests that the constraints are not solely external. The researcher's own cultural and linguistic knowledge, disciplinary affiliations and financial and logistic resources also serve as important determinants of the choice of topic, the country mix, the contextual variables and the approach adopted.

Cross-national comparisons afford a powerful test of objectivity not only because researchers may have a blinkered view of their own society and be convinced that theirs is the best way, but also because they may seek to analyse practices in different cultural settings through their own (inappropriate) conceptual lens. Inevitably, researchers have their own culturally and linguistically determined assumptions and their own mindsets. The experience of being engaged in comparative work may enable them to see the familiar from a new perspective and to become more receptive to differences. As outsiders, they may even be able to gain an understanding of phenomena that was not obvious to insiders.

Kinnear (1987) has shown, for example, how the problems of interference of the researcher's own background affected all aspects of comparative studies that crossed the East–West ideological divide during the period of the Cold War in Europe. Tennom (1995) has compared the way in which the research environment in two neighbouring West European countries, Britain and France, informs attitudes towards international co-operation. Due to their status as civil servants, French social science researchers are protected from external interference, which is an important factor explaining why they are able to concentrate on fundamental research, theoretical and conceptual work, and the production of new knowledge, isolated from the major economic, political and social concerns of the day. They are not dependent on external funding or driven by the market demands for output, unlike their British counterparts, who are forced to concentrate on applied, policy-relevant research and the user interface. While French researchers tend to operate in a closed self-contained world of discourse and debate, British researchers, with their undoubted advantage of possessing an international language as their mother tongue, are likely to hold an Anglocentric view of the world and to expect other research communities to adopt their *modus operandi* in international networks. The obstacles to international co-operation and understanding between Britain and France are, thus, considerable and help to explain the preference in many of the cross-national studies carried out by British researchers for cross-Atlantic or Antipodean, rather than cross-Channel, partners.

Differences in the cultural backgrounds of researchers reflect what have long been identified as disparities in intellectual styles. In the early 1980s,

Galtung (1982) distinguished between three intellectual styles in the West: Saxonic, Teutonic and Gallic. The Teutonic and Gallic styles were characterised by their interest in exploration, theory and explanation with differences in emphasis, and the Saxonic by its attention to description and empiricism. Similar characteristics have been identified in the socio-political traditions of the three countries. Desrosières (1996) has shown how differences in political styles influence national statistical systems: Britain is recognised for its empiricism and a much less codified system, described as 'political arithmetic', German legalism has rooted statistics in the formal description of states, while French centralism and cartesianism have resulted in a high level of legitimacy being attributed to statistical institutions. These differences in intellectual traditions and research cultures are found to result in disparities among the categories used to collect and analyse data and, consequently, in their comparability. Differences can, as Desrosières argues, become an object of study in their own right and a source of information about the underlying social structures.

Equivalence of concepts across contexts

In all research, concepts or the ideas or meaning conveyed by a term are the pegs or reference points for identifying and grouping phenomena. For Dogan and Pelassy (1990: 24), 'there can be no comparisons without concepts'. Rose (1991) makes the point that, in political science, they serve as categories for collecting and sorting information and that it is the operationalization of concepts that enables theories to be tested by empirical observations.

In research that crosses cultural and linguistic boundaries, following on from the examples in the previous section, analysis of the social construction of concepts is an essential component in the characterization of national systems. Many concepts do not, however, travel well across national boundaries, and the question of the equivalence of concepts in different contexts has become a central issue in cross-national comparisons. Desrosières (1996) selects the French *cadre, corps d'ingénieurs* or *grandes écoles* as examples of problems in identifying conceptual equivalence. Levine (1987) shows how differences, in the way attitudes towards time are conceptualized, affect perceptions of what may be considered tactless, dishonest or impolite in one culture but is accepted as standard practice in another. Hyman (1998: 52) has stressed how even the central concepts in the area of industrial relations (trade union, *Gewerkschaft, syndicat, sindicato*) vary in their functions and significance across nations but, goes on to show the interest of analysing issues presenting equivalent challenges to union identities in different national contexts. Eyraud and Rychener (1986: 210) have stressed the importance of looking beyond job titles at their content and the social processes that shape it. Rose (1991: 447) takes the example of the British Prime Minister, the German *Bundeskanzler*, the Italian *Presidente del Consiglio dei Ministri* and the Irish *Taoiseach*, as functionally equivalent units providing a suitable grouping for comparative analysis and as 'sufficiently abstract to travel across national boundaries'. His argument might have been more difficult to sustain had he included the French *Premier ministre*, given the more powerful role played by the presidency in the Fifth Republic and its overshadowing of the premiership. Dogan and Pelassy (1990: 37) have illustrated the problems of identifying functional equivalence by pointing out that the three different functions of the French President are fulfilled by two officials in the UK and by three in Italy. Although the meaning of many of the key concepts in social policy – training, unemployment, take-up of benefits, part-time work, flexibility, parental leave, childcare, reconciliation of paid and unpaid work, lone parenthood, equality, mainstreaming – may be contested across EU member states, they can offer a valuable unit for cross-national societal analysis, if researchers look beyond the encoding, and use them as a starting point (Hantrais and Letablier 1996, Hantrais 1999b, 2000). Many more examples of the problems of dealing with contextual, conceptual and functional equivalence are described in the other contributions to this volume.

Interpretation and evaluation

The material presented in this paper suggests there is no single recipe, or one best way, for carrying out cross-national comparisons. Just as inputs and products of cross-national projects are many and varied, so are the methods. In the same way that cross-national studies reveal how similar and different processes may lead to similar findings about social phenomena (universal trends and convergence), or how similar or different processes may produce different results (cultural diversity and divergence), the inputs and outcomes of the cross-national research process may also converge or diverge. Perhaps cross-national methods can be most accurately depicted as representing a meal from an *à la carte* menu, where individual researchers select according to their tastes and expertise, the time and funding they have available, and the results they are seeking to achieve. The less experienced or less well resourced researchers, eating alone or in small groups, may want to limit their meal to two courses, while the weight watcher will exercise caution in selecting a properly balanced diet and pay careful attention to the ingredients. The more confident, adventurous and better resourced international team of researchers may opt for a full fixed menu, able to accommodate individual tastes, preferences, diets and constraints. The restaurant will be selected for its reliability and value for money. Each member of the team will bring to the meal a different range of experiences and expectations, and also culturally determined table manners. Subsequent reports on the event will reflect individual reactions to the quality and quantity of the food and wine served, and the blending of the ingredients and dishes.

An extension of this culinary metaphor can be used to elucidate the interactive relationship in the cross-national research process between the researcher and the method adopted. The availability and quality of the ingredients (concepts and data) vary from one restaurant (country or society) to another, but so do the preferred recipes (methods) and menus (social constructions) that go to make up the meal (research project). The experience and skills of the cooks (researchers), the restaurant manager (team leader), their tastes (cultural backgrounds and prejudices) will determine whether they opt for a menu aimed at mass consumption, whether they try to satisfy a specialized clientèle, or whether they offer a more varied bill of fare designed to address the needs of different users. Whatever the option chosen, the restaurant owners (sponsors) will expect to see a reasonable return on their investment.

From the experience of eating in one restaurant, or even twenty restaurants, it would clearly be dangerous to conclude that all restaurants, or a subset of them, are good or bad. If two clients who have eaten the same dish both suffer from food poisoning the next day, it would be tempting to deduce that the dish was the cause of the upset, but if another client did not have the same symptoms, a larger number of factors would have to be investigated. Explaining why a particular restaurant chain can, or cannot, be successfully transported across national borders is not simply an academic question. It requires all the skills of the experienced cross-national comparative researcher to carry out careful scrutiny of a wide range of socio-economic, political, national and local factors and to interpret and evaluate the findings with due regard for the cultural bias of his/her own background.

Notes

1. French authors (Maurice 1989, for example) have followed Grootings' distinction and, in the absence of direct equivalents in French, have used the English terminology in doing so. The two approaches identified by Grootings are, thus, subsumed within the generic term *comparaisons internationales*. The adjective *interculturelles* is occasionally added to refer to studies that emphasize the cultural dimension (Schultheis 1991), and the *effet sociétal* is used by Maurice to refer to a more elaborate version of 'international' comparisons where macro and micro-level phenomena are treated as integrated units of analysis.
2. Sociological textbooks and dictionaries (Jary and Jary 1991, for example) most often refer to cross-cultural comparisons or cross-societal analysis. The journal of comparative social science by Sage has its title as *Cross-Cultural Research*, implying a catch-all term, 'spanning societies, nations and cultures'.

References

Allsopp, V. (1995) *Understanding Economics* (London: Routledge).

Byrne, P. (ed.) (1999) The Changing Political Environment. *Cross-National Research Papers*, **5**(2).

Corden, A. and Duffy, K. (1998) Human dignity and social exclusion. In R. Sykes and P. Alcock (eds) *Developments in European Social Policy* (Bristol: The Policy Press), pp 95–124.

Desrosières, A. (1996) Statistical traditions: an obstacle to international comparisons? In L. Hantrais and S. Mangen (eds), *Cross-National Research Methods in the Social Sciences* (London: Pinter), pp 17–27.

Dogan, M. and Pelassy, D. (1990) *How to Compare Nations: Strategies in Comparative Politics* (Second Edition) (Chatham, New Jersey: Chatham House Publishers).

Eardley, T. (1996) Lessons from a study of social assistance schemes in the OECD countries. In L. Hantrais and S. Mangen (eds) *Cross-National Research Methods in the Social Sciences* (London: Pinter), pp 51–62.

Esping-Andersen, G. (1990) *The Three Worlds of Welfare Capitalism* (Oxford: Polity Press).

Esping-Andersen, G. (ed.) (1996) *Welfare States in Transition: National Adaptations in Global Economies* (London: Sage).

Eyraud, F. and Rychener, F. (1986) A societal analysis of new technologies. In P. Grootings (ed.) *Technology and Work. East-West Comparison* (London: Croom Helm), pp 209–230.

Galtung, J. (1982) On the meaning of 'nation' as a 'variable'. In M. Niessen and J. Peschar (eds) *International Comparative Research. Problems of Theory, Methodology and Organization in Eastern and Western Europe* (Oxford: Pergamon), pp 17–34.

Grootings, P. (1986) Technology and work: a topic for East-West comparison? In P. Grootings (ed.) *Technology and Work. East-West Comparison* (London: Croom Helm), pp 275–301.

Green, N.L. (1994) The comparative method and postructural structuralism–new perspectives for migration studies. *Journal of American Ethnic History*, **13**(4), 3–22.

Hantrais, L. (ed.) (1999a) Changing Gender Relations. *Cross-National Research Papers*, **5**(3).

Hantrais, L. (ed.) (2000) *Gendered Policies in Europe: Reconciling Employment and Family Life* (London: Macmillan).

Hantrais, L. (ed.) (1999b) Interactions between Socio-Demographic Trends, Social and Economic Policies. *Cross-National Research Papers*, **5**(1).

Hantrais, L. and Mangen, S. (eds) (1996) *Cross-National Research Methods in the Social Sciences* (London: Pinter).

Hantrais, L. and Letablier, M-T. (1996) *Families and Family Policies in Europe* (London: Longman).

Hantrais, L. and Lohkamp-Himmighofen, M. (eds) (1999) Changing Family Forms, Law and Policy. *Cross-National Research Papers*, **5**(3).

Hantrais, L., and Sineau, M. (with B. Lust) (1998) *L'administration du travail: acteur privilégié d'une politique d'égalité professionnelle entre les femmes et les hommes. Guide de bonnes pratiques.* Document n° 55–1 (Geneva: Bureau International du Travail).

Hyman, R. (1998) Recherche sur les syndicats et comparaison internationale, *Revue de l'IRES*, n° 28, Special issue, 43–61.

Jary, D. and Jary, J. (1991) *Collins Dictionary of Sociology* (Glasgow: Harper Collins).

Jones Finer, C. (1999) Trends and developments in welfare states. In J. Clasen, (ed.) *Comparative Social Policy: Concepts, Theories and Methods* (Oxford: Blackwell), pp 15–33.

Jobert, A. (1996) Comparing education, training and employment in Germany, the United Kingdom and Italy. In L. Hantrais and S. Mangen (eds) *Cross-National Research Methods in the Social Sciences* (London: Pinter), pp 76–83.

Kinnear, R. (1987) Interference from the researcher's background in comparisons across the ideological divide. *Cross-National Research Papers*, **1**(4), 9–14.

Lammers, C.J. and Hickson, D.J. (1979) *Organizations Alike and Unlike: International and Inter-Institutional Studies in the Sociology of Organizations* (London and Henley: Routledge and Kegan Paul).

Levine, R.V. (1987) Coping with the silent language in cross-national research. *Cross-National Research Papers*, **1**(3), 27–33.

Lim, L.L. (1996) *More and Better Jobs for Women. An Action Guide* (Geneva: International Labour Office).

Maurice, M. (1989) Méthode comparative et analyse sociétale. Les implications théoriques des comparaisons internationales. *Sociologie du travail*, n° 2, 175–191.

Mishra, R. (1984) *The Welfare State in Crisis?* (Brighton: Wheatsheaf).

Øyen, E. (1990) The imperfections of comparisons. In E. Øyen (ed.) *Comparative Methodology. Theory and Practice in International Social Research* (London: Sage), pp 1–18.

Przeworski, A. and Teune, H. (1970) *The Logic of Comparative Social Inquiry* (New York: John Wiley).

Riley, M. (1963) *Sociological Research: A Case Approach*, vol. 1 (New York: Harcourt Brace and World).

Robinson, W. (1951) The logical structure of analytical induction, *American Sociological Review*, **16**(6), 812–819.

Rose, M. (1985) Universalism, culturalism and the Aix group: promise and problems of a societal approach to economic institutions. *European Sociological Review*, **1**(1), 65–83.

Rose, R. (1991) Comparing forms of comparative analysis. *Political Studies*, **39**(3), 446–462.

Schultheis, F. (1991) Introduction. In F. de Singly and F. Schultheis (eds) *Affaires de famille, affaires d'État: sociologie de la famille* (Jarville-La-Malgrange: Éditions de l'Est), pp 5–22.

Schunk, M. (1996) Constructing models of the welfare mix: care options of frail elders. In L. Hantrais
    and S. Mangen (eds) *Cross-National Research Methods in the Social Sciences* (London: Pinter), pp
    84–94.
Tennom, J. (1995) European research communities: France vs. the United Kingdom. *The Puzzle of
    Integration. European Yearbook on Youth Policy and Research* (CYRCE), **1,** 269–281.
Teune, H. (1990) Comparing countries: lessons learned. In E. Øyen (ed.) *Comparative Methodology.
    Theory and Practice in International Social Research* (London: Sage), pp 38–62.
Wilensky, H. and Lebeaux, C. (1958) *Industrial Society and Welfare* (New York: Free Press).

Qualitative research methods in cross-national settings

STEEN MANGEN

Introduction

This article discusses the impact of research objectives, and theoretical and conceptual problems on decisions concerning the design of qualitative cross-national investigations, whether they be cross-cultural, multilingual, or a single-country analysis undertaken by a non-native. As qualitative research texts tend to underplay the cross-national dimension, and cross-national research texts are generally scanty in their depiction of qualitative methods, many of the examples of good practice, as well as caveats, come from *Cross-National Research Papers*, which have been published since 1985.[1]

There is a view – rejected here – that qualitative research is at the softer end of the methodological spectrum and is vitiated by unrigorous application. Equally, to be rejected is the idea that qualitative methods are somehow preliminary to other, quantified analyses. In this regard, Silverman (1993) juxtaposes the positivist prioritizing of quantitative hypothesis testing, by examining mechanistic correlations between variables, and the interpretivist tradition which is primarily concerned with hypothesis generation. But, one can certainly argue along the lines of Hakim (1987) that the qualitative approach, when theoretically informed, is the most open-ended, flexible, exploratory means of formulating hypotheses for further structured analysis.

Narrative and documentary material form the essence of qualitative research, whether this is collected via a pre-structured or relatively

Steen Mangen is Lecturer in European Social Policy at the London School of Economics and Political Science, Houghton Street, London WC2A 2AE, UK. He specializes in research on welfare states in Spain and Germany, as well as European urban development. His recent publications include (edited with Linda Hantrais) *Cross-National Research Methods in the Social Sciences* (Pinter, 1996).

unstructured ethnographic strategy. The majority of the investigations cited here are typical of the bias in research effort in the policy arena in being principally concerned with policy process and outcomes on the clientèle. Whatever their focus, their results reinforce the argument that the difficult task of explanation and interpretation in cross-national environments demands that investigators be sensitized to multifarious historical, cultural and political specificities (May 1993; Hantrais in this issue). The need to locate phenomena in dynamic societal contexts – and, in particular, to show how endogenous and exogenous variables may interact – is, arguably, even more pressing in qualitative contexts and poses a major challenge to the cross-national application of measurement instruments.

The potential of the qualitative approach in cross-national settings

Qualitative research is not simply non-numerical. Its central defence lies in its ability to penetrate the experiential social worlds of intentional, self-directing actors, whether through the spoken or written word. Strauss and Corbin (1990) advance the primacy of the individual's narrative accounts for the grounding of theory: in its focus on social process, it is the person's own account that matters. Such an insistence can, within cross-national projects, counteract what Coffey and Atkinson (1996) have termed the 'culture of fragmentation' that is characteristic of analyses derived from heavily precoded and categorized data.

To summarize, the strengths of qualitative approaches lie in attempts to reconcile complexity, detail and context. Critical for protagonists is the integration of 'reflexivity', by which is meant the ability of researchers to take stock of their actions and their role in the research process. This is a particularly urgent task in research crossing cultural boundaries. Flexibility, too, is a definite asset. Mason (1996), for example, makes the important point that research strategies may be introduced sequentially: for example, the design of interviews may be contingent on prior analysis of documentary material. The issue of flexibility is linked to the practicality of investigator and methodological triangulation. Yet, Silverman (1993) cautions about the seductive charms of an unreflective use of the qualitative method. The respondent's interpretation may not represent a reasoned explanation. This may be particularly relevant in 'expert' interviews, where the researcher may be seeking guidance with regard to the problematic, as well as using the interviews to collect data. Silverman offers advice on how to cope with the fact that the phenomenon always escapes complete understanding via efforts at wide contextualization; and he urges the avoidance of electing between polar explanatory opposites, and advocates multifactorial explanation. In particular, he is critical of naive 'touristic' approaches that stereotype the results. Bryman (1988) contributes to these concerns by insisting that, in eschewing a predetermined research structure, we are not lured into avoiding engaging in the analytic act: at the end of the day, hypotheses must be tested against some explicit criteria.

As opposed to the ideal type adumbrated above, much cross-national research involves pragmatic accommodations. Linguistic competences and comparative lack of familiarity with other cultures compromise these ambitions. One coping strategy is to redouble efforts at triangulation, in part through a 'saturation' tactic of combining qualitative and quantitative methods. At the least, this should extend the contextual reliability of our analyses by enhancing our capacity to interpret the more impersonal statistical data.[2] At preliminary stages of investigation, a useful exploitation of this pragmatic approach, although not without criticism of the dangers of descent into impressionistic interpretation, is the 'safari method'. Its use is largely indicated where problems are being examined which are relatively well-specified cross-nationally, and for which surveys and national data may be reasonably available for secondary analysis, matched by opportunities for personal observation and 'expert' interviews.

The rest of the paper reviews the problems of working in foreign languages, before discussing critical issues of sampling and reviewing cross-national implications of the most common qualitative methods.

The problem of language

Each language is not only a medium for intercourse but a particular style of discourse. Thus, the linguistic dimension interacts with cultural, as well as associated intellectual and professional specificities to form the problematic of comparative analysis. The ultimate challenge is to make sense of cognitive, connotational and functional meanings.[3] The fact that most comparative research is also multidisciplinary only serves to complicate the task (Hantrais and Ager 1985, Lisle 1985).

Yet, issues of linguistic competence tend to be downgraded in much cross-national qualitative research. This is all the more curious, given the almost insurmountable task in translation to do with figures of speech – metaphor, litotes, aphorisms, euphemisms, hyperbole, innuendo, irony, and so on – as well as dialect and non-verbal cues. As a partial remedy, van de Vijver and Kwok Leung (1997) consider solutions to problems of 'construct' and 'item' bias, noting in passing the cultural variation of responses to analogies and concrete definitions.

The difficulties of working in more than one language are especially acute in interpersonal research aiming to examine emotional responses. Where languages and cultural contexts are 'near neighbours', one may come close to a resolution. In their study of cultures, care and life histories, Chamberlayne and King (1996), both functionally bilingual in German and English, embarked on an elaborate method embracing narrative interviews, hermeneutic textual analysis and thematic field analysis. In the Anglo-Indian project reported by Leff (1985), the team anticipated problems of achieving contextual equivalence from the cross-national interpretation of differential lexicons of emotion. In an experiment, a third bilingual investigator, who was an Indian, had access to tape recordings only, whereas his colleagues had engaged in interviewing. While, overall, reliability was acceptable, a particular deficiency was the interpretation of emotional warmth, where the third investigator's bilingual ratings were closer to those of his Indian compatriot than the British. Knowledge of a particular language, then, may be a necessary but by no means sufficient requisite for cultural understanding and the achievement of functional and conceptual equivalence. The *Cross-National Research Papers* provide ample evidence of the obstacles to achieving linguistic equivalence in seemingly unproblematic terms like 'part-time work', 'household' and 'single person'. The problems are compounded at the conceptual level when attempting to cope cross-nationally with phenomena like 'welfare state' or 'inner city'.[4] Lawrence (1988) refers to the dangers of the 'fallacy of self-fulfilling equivalence', in situations where one is tempted to impose consonant definitions on disparate phenomena. The investigation of Soviet child care by Harwin (1987) is a case in point, in alerting us to this situation. 'Child care' and 'social work' proved problematic for translation, but functional equivalence was also difficult to achieve: Soviet child inspectors, whilst superficially performing similar duties to UK social workers, operated with a different focus, primarily oriented to the child rather than the family, and practised in a context of substantially different values and knowledge base.

Several authors in this volume, in our edited collection (Hantrais and Mangen 1996) and in the *Cross-National Research Papers*, have addressed managerial and analytic issues when dealing with multilingual research. Lisle (1985), for example, urges the employment of bilateral analyses of the relevant languages, rather than a reduction to one language, in order to construct what he terms a 'polygonal synthesis'. Along similar lines, Ungerson (1996) is occupied with linguistic dimensions in grounded theory: the language of the presentation of findings can lock in analysis to a particular logic or structure, with a loss of meaning and nuance arising from the translation of direct quotation. For her, monolingual publication will conceal the culturally-loaded meanings of interview material derived from several languages into a very partial explanatory key. One, albeit imperfect solution, is the retention of multilingualism at the writing-up stage. This strategy – as with that of Lisle – may, however, be significantly constrained by resource scarcities.

There can be no doubt that the use of one language in multilingual environments imposes serious limits. Yet, research is essentially a social – and political – act, and in many international projects dictates outside the purely scientific impose severe constraints on methodological design. One issue is aegis, that is, organizational or financial sponsorship, which is briefly discussed later. Of more relevance here is the frequent situation where researchers may have outstanding subject expertise unmatched by linguistic competence. Many 'expert reports' published under the aegis of international organizations fall into this category. Given these constraints, how can difficulties be minimized? Harding (1996), for example, attempts to limit language barriers by tactical sampling. In his study of urban governance, he consciously selected only northern European countries for which there was wide availability of relevant English-language literature. But he admits that he had to make compromises which have affected his command over his data: heavy dependence on 'expert' interviews with English speakers and, given the relative expense, limited translation of essential contextual documentation.

Yet, even impressive competence in English on the part of foreign respondents can prove deceptive and, moreover, may introduce certain ethical considerations in research terms. Lawrence (1988) insists that the linguistic onus should be on researchers rather than respondents, for it is the former who are gaining from the enterprise. Respondents, typically have to make on-the-spot decisions about what is being asked of them, particularly where questions are open to several nuances, or contain linguistic 'false friends'. For example, he cites the different meaning of 'agenda' in Dutch (diary) and English (work or policy schedule). For this reason, he urges us to interview in the informant's language even when we are not fluent. But, where the language of the respondent is simply beyond us, he suggests the exploitation of extensive translation of the key vocabulary. In a similar vein, in cross-cultural research on sexual behaviour conducted among ethnic minorities in the UK, Bowler (1997) found that even a superficial knowledge of key terms in the relevant subcontinental languages assisted understanding and, just as importantly, established rapport with interviewees. Equally, however, she speculates on the intrusive impact of bilingual interviewers who she needed to assist her, particularly with regard to their vital role in explaining what, in a culturally sensitive area, was required of the respondents.

Faced with pragmatic compromises in language management, it behoves the investigator to engage in a cost-benefit analysis of the project's intellectual potential at the planning stage and, if it proceeds, to disseminate this assessment with the presentation of findings.

Problems of sampling

Ethnographic researchers tend to eschew sampling and treat whole narrative or textual analyses as legitimate objects in their own right. In other types of cross-national qualitative research, which is typically small scale, the issue of sampling and variable incorporation is to the fore. Here, the limits of space allow only for selective comments. Many researchers have sought a sampling rationale in theoretically driven typologies, which might permit greater scope for generalizable inference, although this does not obviate problems of representativeness of the phenomena under study. Nor can we avoid difficult decisions with regard to selection of key endogenous and exogenous variables, the objective being an appropriate trade-off between empirical 'extension' and analytic 'intension' (Sartori 1978). For his part, Manning (1993) is critical of over-reliance on 'most similar' typologies which have been narrowly drawn because they may eliminate much of the key constellation of variables where the interesting variance may be located.

To resolve the multi-faceted problems of sampling, several studies reported in this volume have resorted to the 'snowballing' technique. Only in the most propitious of circumstances does this avoid *ad hoc* revisions to sampling strategy which compromise representativity. Zulauf (in this issue) admits that this technique required her to expand the dependent variable (in her case, work status), prolonging and increasing the cost of sampling, in part due to a dependency on national collaborators to identify people possessing the relevant criteria.

Given that samples are typically restricted, issues related to the selection of the unit of analysis are paramount. Cross-national systemic research is beyond most researchers' capacities to execute effectively and solely by qualitative methods. However, these issues apart, questions arise about the appropriateness of national or sub-national units of analysis in highly differentiated countries. Harwin (1987) records her frustrations at having to opt for one sub-national location in the then USSR, where pervasive differences existed between the urban and rural.

Finally, the consequences arising from 'aegis' have been noted in sampling and the selection of units of analysis. Zulauf, in this volume, in her discussion of single-person research, takes up these issues in terms of the employing organization and receptiveness to her particular nationality. More generally, many European union (EU)-funded projects require that all member states be included or, at least, impose participation of 'Cohesion Fund' countries or 'Objective 1' regions, whereas, on valid empirical grounds, it may have been more justifiable to restrict the sample or to include non-EU states. Official sponsorship can also impose serious constraints. Harwin (1987) admits that, although the aegis of Soviet officialdom gave her speedy access to some of her material, the conditions imposed—largely due to bureaucratic compartmentalization—restricted incorporation of other sources. In her case, problems were exacerbated by the pervasiveness of a 'non specific distrust' of Westerners coming to undertake research in the East.

Management strategies

Since the early 1980s, a variety of international networking techniques have been adopted, not least in response to the growing research agenda of EU institutions. Two principal manifestations are dedicated teams engaged on particular topics and the convocation of seminars with varying degrees of formalization. In this regard, Millar (1990) describes a study of the social situation of single women. She adopted what is becoming a conventional team approach: the production of parallel national state-of-the-art expert reports according to predetermined guidelines, complemented by special thematic reports and exploitation of existing EU databases such as the Labour Force or Household Panel surveys. For Millar, reliance on national reports is often the only effective means for the rapid generation of a large array of comparable data, although she acknowledges that parallel methods typically fall short of the ideal: common predetermined guidelines were varyingly interpreted according to local exigencies and differences in academic priorities.

Other projects may not be so well endowed. Faced with limited resources, Bastard and his two colleagues (1989) eschewed the formulation of a common approach to the study of divorce and, instead, attempted to maximize their collective knowledge of three states by utilizing each other's techniques in their own countries. This method, they argue, is cheap and effective in forcing each investigator to look afresh at situations which, through familiarity, had lost their intellectual force as part of the problematic.

The potential for cross-national collaboration has been enhanced by the sponsorship of regular targeted seminars, not least by EU institutions. These venues have the obvious advantage of being less time consuming and are a cheaper means of exploiting expertise. As ever, they offer opportunities. They are advanced by Letablier and Beechey (1989), for example, as a valued *modus operandi* in permitting open discussion of different intellectual priorities and focuses. But important considerations may be needed to be resolved, including the problem of which actors provide the lead to maintain the momentum, and the consequences this can carry for dictating the primary research agenda (Warman and Millar 1996).

A selective review of qualitative methods

By its very nature, cross-national research typically extracts greater methodological compromises than a single-country focus. Commonly, investigators have sought, where possible, to improve design by integrating different methods. Hakim (1987) helpfully outlines overlaps between modes of investigation (designs which merge the characterisitics of two methodological types), the potential for linking two studies, and situations where studies can be combined. Of course, whatever the investigative mode, each generates its own issues concerning reliability and validity. In this regard, both Silverman (1993) and Creswell (1998) are particularly insightful in providing a structured critique of the major approaches.

This review of cross-national research methods is by no means exhaustive.[5] There is no space here to consider secondary analysis, group or focus group interviews, panel data derived from diaries, biographies, time series or longitudinal studies, and so forth. The methods that are reviewed – case studies, surveys using questionnaires or interviews, documentary research and quasi-experimental methods – are, of course, not mutually exclusive.

Case studies

The case study is essentially an analytical focus rather than a method *per se*, since it commonly incorporates several approaches, a combination of interviews and documentary research being the most typical in cross-national research. Many primarily qualitative case studies also rely on quantitative data to round off the attempt to obtain a sensitive and multi-dimensional perspective of the situation or event under study.

Certain academic disciplines, not least history, espouse the primacy of the critical case study as the fundamental explanatory model and a justifiable end in itself, and by no means preliminary to larger scale techniques. Certainly, the case study remains central to cross-national theoretical development. Defenders of the exclusivity of the model cite the unique constellation of factors in each country which cannot be forced into a standardized comparative analysis without serious loss of meaning. They argue that standardized approaches to social phenomena have tended to stimulate unproductive, competitive testing of macrolevel theories – in welfare state research, for example, which has privileged either moderniza-tion/convergence or 'politics matter' arguments – whereas more valid explanation may lie in pursuing the complementarity of different models (Mabbett and Bolderson 1999).

However, the uniqueness argument is double-edged: case studies that are restricted to a single country can only be regarded as addressing a comparative problematic if they apply hypotheses which, by implication, extend to phenomena beyond the case country (Dogan and Pelassy 1984). For his part, Stake (1998) encourages us not to concentrate on the comparative dimension in seeking to make sense of case study material, and asserts that generalizations derived from observations of differences in two cases may well be less valid than generalizations derived from a single study.

Surveys

Apart from case studies one-off surveys are the most common qualitative approach, particularly where the research is being undertaken by a single person. Regular or continuous sample surveys undertaken, for example, by Eurostat may also provide valuable contextual material (see Harkness and Singleton in this issue). As discussed earlier, the critical concern with surveys undertaken in different cultures is the verification that an acceptable level of equivalence of meaning in concept, context and function has been established. Several investigators point to the constant dangers that survey methods may be tapping into different elements of a given phenemenon in each culture without gathering in the whole, particularly if they are constructed within one dominant cultural or linguistic perspective (see the collection edited by Harkness 1998). This is particularly a risk in fixed questionnaires eliciting semantic differentials in attitudes (May 1993). Over-rigid or inappropriate questionnaire design, then, can trap meaning. To these problems must be added the difficulties arising in situations where cultural propensities to complete questionnaires or familiarity with them is low. Bowler (1997), for example, notes the problems she incurred in attempting to administer self-completed questionnaires on sexual practices among ethnic minorities in the UK originating from the subcontinent. The high level of guidance required from the investigators negated the purpose of the exercise.

Several investigators offer risk minimization tactics from their own research. Although cost may be a vital consideration, Hantrais (1989) recommends the use of batteries of questions, rather than reliance on single items, especially in situations where there is the possibility to derive constructs from integrating indirect subjective and objective indicators. This also affords the investigator greater leverage in searching for patterns or clusters of responses for further analysis. Data disaggregation is also proposed. Roy (1989) relates how she was able to overcome rigid closed definitions in questions derived from the EU Labour Force Survey by supplementing time-budget data which allows for a disaggregation and reconstruction of labour market data. Closed questionnaire data were supplemented by semi-directed, in-depth interviews in a study of leisure time and women's relations to paid work described by Le Feuvre (1989), which allowed the investigators to infuse key cultural specificities.

Semi-structured and 'measured' free-format interview schedules are the most common media employed in cross-national survey research. As a generalization, it has to be said that interviews are high-risk ventures which require detailed planning. Zulauf's frustrations, described in this issue, arising from differential cultural propensities to respond to introductory letters are an experience shared by many researchers. The alternative tactic of 'phoning cold' proved more profitable for her, albeit personally less comfortable. Of course, receptivity to telephone requests also varies among cultures and its feasibility is, ultimately, determined by the density of the network.

In most cross-national research settings, data collection costs are high, since interviews are expensive to set up and are typically non-repeatable. Unless linguistic competence is extensive, and much contextual research has been completed in advance, the researcher would be ill advised to opt for a highly unstructured interviews, thus limiting the ability to exploit the full potential of the interpretive qualitative method. Furthermore, unstructured interviews, if they are to render sufficient data, tend to be very time consuming, and they raise ethical considerations of the overblown expectations of the respondents on the part of the interviewer, especially in research projects that do not allow an element of reciprocity.

In general, the foreign interviewer is in a much more non-directive, passive position than a native, and this must be taken into consideration in assessing the quality of the material collected, for example in identifying possible 'halo effects'. Interviewing in a second language is strenuous, because it quickly exposes any weakness of linguistic or cultural competence. Requesting clarification of colloquialisms, and so forth, can prove tedious and can antagonize respondents by interrupting the flow of their discourse, although this may be less of a constraint in 'expert' interviews.

Clearly, many problems could be overcome by tape recordings where repeated hearings of interviews, assisted perhaps by native speakers, could resolve difficulties. It could also prevent the distractions to both interviewer and respondent of note-taking or coding on the spot. But the danger also exists that recording can inhibit respondents or cause them to decline to participate: some cultures are not attuned to non-official interviews at all, especially when they are being recorded; and in 'expert' interviews there may be the added possibility of respondents' concern about the attribution of material being collected.

The different status of the interviewer and respondent may need to be taken into account in determining the location of the interview. Many respondents are naturally sensitive to the potential of a foreign interviewer swanning in to ask intimate questions about sexual behaviour, alcohol intake and so on, and the data collected are at risk of a substantial halo effect. Where interviewers do not share the language, nationality, gender, status or age of the respondent and are posing personal questions, there is a good case for selecting a neutral venue under the aegis of a local organization.

Different consequences stem from seeking the co-operation of the public and relying on 'expert' interviews, the latter being particularly common in cross-national research, where often it is not only primary data that is required but also guidance and a local gatekeeper to networks of appropriate informants. One advantage of 'expert' interviews in cross-national research is that they tend to be easier to obtain and, on balance, the risk of linguistic or cultural distortion effects is smaller. On the other hand, representativity of the sample is again an issue. Moreover, as Deacon (1987) discovered in his study of opinions about welfare in Hungary, expert responses may essentially reflect official discourse rather than personal opinion or actual behaviour.

Elite and expert interviews may carry a high risk of cancellation or curtailment, and efforts should be made to factor this into project management. These considerations, of course, are not restricted to cross-national projects, but are likely to be at a premium, given the likely higher costs of achieving a completed interview. It is, for instance, vital to prioritize the themes that are most important to address first. Also important is the contextualization of material in advance as a prompt, especially if referring to non-contemporary events, or where the particular research problems are not high on the agenda of the country being analysed. When expert and elite interviews are being planned during the working week, and data refer to events evolving over time and are conducted under time pressure (for example, a maximum of one hour allotted) and with interruptions, such as phone calls, a case can be made for sending in advance an outline of the research protocol and the sort of material required. Of course, the pros and cons of adopting this strategy must be calculated, especially in situations where respondents may be alerted to an underlying critical stance and, hence, may be afforded time to prepare 'set' answers.

Documentary research

Documentary methods may be seriously open to the danger that material has already been highly edited and structured for purposes extraneous to the research project. Given that documents are produced in specific cultural and subcultural contexts, it is even more difficult for the cross-national investigator to assess this impact in interpreting data. The aegis of the document is an important consideration: in general, reports authored by pressure groups, for example, are *per se* critical of official policy, whereas public documents may pursue a conservative line and will be based on 'measurement by fiat', which can obfuscate meaning (Cicourel 1964).

Nonetheless, a tactical advantage of the method in a cross-national setting is its comparative cheapness, the researcher's ability to set their own workpace and flexibility of manipulation. These include ease of re-consultation and re-analysis, disaggregation of whole texts via content or textual analysis or decisions, where appropriate, to opt for categorical or cross-section editing, assistance with translation, ability to combine material with contextualizing interviews, and so forth. Official reports are more accessible than 'grey' literature which is, by definition, written for a relatively small and 'knowing' audience and whose content may, therefore, be difficult for a foreign researcher to assess. Yet, in small-scale research, it is likely that the latter will be of greater value.

'Grey' literature has been combined with 'expert' and consumer interviews to systematize the mapping of local policy networks. This was the case in respect of a five-country study of inner city regeneration whose ultimate objective was the construction of a large-scale qualitative database (Mangen 1992). Schunk (1996) in a two-country comparison utilized primary documents, participatory observation and in-depth interviews to construct a map of the 'welfare mix' in provisions for elder care.

Quasi-experimental methods

In comparative social research, controlled prospective random studies employing experimental methods have, for obvious reasons, been less often employed, although they could have considerable potential (for example, comparative investigations of policing strategies of narcotics). One simulation model that appears to offer considerable scope for relatively easy further exploitation is the vignette, a helpful brief evaluation of which is provided by Miles and Huberman (1994). The method was used successfully in comparative studies of social work case management described by Cooper and colleagues (1995) and Soydan (1996). However, the vignette method may work best with specialist samples. It is telling that both studies involved professionals. Despite the undoubted professional cultural differences outlined by Ramon (1987), there is some evidence of a higher level of shared practice – in this case among social workers – than among academics. This appears to be the conclusion of the project reported by Warman and Millar (1996), in which the vignette approach was the least successful part of the research design. The international assessment team, investigating family care, found that they could not effectively respond to the situations posed in the vignettes without the hypothetical details being specified down to the smallest detail. The collaborators confessed that they were unclear about what kind of response was being elicited and argued that, for more valid evaluation, an input from practitioners was essential.

Signposts to the future

Mass circulation printed and audio-visual media are being increasingly adopted as a database. In fact, newspapers – articles, advertisements, notices and readers' letters – have a long tradition of forming the basis of local historical research, as Bendikat (1996) demonstrates. But, she also notes, these can be a highly time-consuming source. The investigator may be required to elaborate an on-going schema for structuring material, and the research may incur lengthy stays *in situ*, since many newspapers and magazines have only local circulation. Beyond the printed press, growing interest has been expressed in promotional literature. Silverman (1993), for example, advocates the use of the textual analysis of health promotion packages, which he effectively used in a cross-national study of HIV/AIDs. Although differences are found in cross-cultural responses, there are strong advocates for greater exploitation of visual data in sociological research (Harper 1998). MacGregor (1993) similarly judges that the relevance of audio-visual material and that extracted from the popular press, in significant ways, offers a premium over official data sources. She argues, in her particular research, that these sources have helped shape the semantics of social exclusion. There are other advantages accruing from reliance on audio-visual material, particularly in solutions to lack of linguistic competences and its effective exploitation through qualitative software packages.

Brief mention should also be made of the potential offered by the burgeoning contemporary material available via the Internet or on CD-rom, despite the fact that, in the case of the former, there are problems of long-term retrieval or appropriate citation of sources that are essentially ephemeral.

Qualitative computer software packages (CAQDAS), which mush-roomed in the 1990s, have greatly expanded opportunities for data processing and analysis. Before alluding briefly to their potential, some preliminary reflections are necessary. Qualitative software comes essen-tially as standardized packages. Whilst they are becoming increasingly sophisticated, Coffey and Atkinson (1996) are concerned about the dangers of 'technological determinism' producing a perverse convergence to the use of a dominant analytical mode, which is a product of the relative dominance of a couple of packages. Although their capabilities are expanding exponentially, CAQDAS may not address primary research or methodo-logical concerns. Frustrations, and possibly alienation from, and lack of command over, data management can arise in situations where the software's logic departs from that of the enquiry.

Packages may incur high initiation costs in terms of data management when related to processing needs, and local IT support may not be available, a problem reinforced by the fact that some of the manuals are clearly written for skilled computer programmers. Moreover basic wordprocessing packages may execute most of the tasks required: this was the case in a trial of 'code and retrieve' procedures undertaken by Stanley and Temple (1996), who valued the ability to work in one medium only and found little purchase in opting for dedicated software packages. Analogous to the dangers of computer analysis of quantitative data for crass number crunching, Richards and Richards (1995) point out that qualitative software can lead to an unreflective generation of non-theoretically grounded categorizations: they give examples of the overprofusion of inappropriate 'trees' or 'nodes' that a misuse of their NUD*IST programme can generate.

With these caveats in mind, there is no doubt of the considerable added value that CAQDAS can offer in speed, and the capacity for comprehensive analytical searching, even with large datasets, without heavy prestructuring or precoding of data. The interaction with other media such as the Internet, or utilization of scanners for rapid and mass entry of written data, and the manipulation via hypermedia point to their value as 'theory building' devices (Coffey and Atkinson 1996). The retention and storage of whole texts on computer can permit serial re-analysis and also allow other researchers to re-interpret the data. The key strength of the newer packages is the ease with which they can produce visual display or relationships between data that may be an essential aid in refining hypotheses. They also offer many routes to the quantification of data, where this is desirable. However, the potential for this sort of manipulation in multilingual projects may only be heightened by the relevant data for this purpose being analysed in one language, with obvious negative consequences.

With regard to grounded theory, programmes like NUD*iST and Atlas-Ti, each in their own way, permit the researcher to develop systematic relationships among categories of data. For example, the authors of the former programme argue that, through its production of hierarchies of generality and specificity, the research enterprise is transformed into a more potentially exciting task: one to do with the construction and exploration of new categories and linkages between them as data can be subcategorized, spliced, linked together to examine more refined patterning or to unravel 'nested' or embedded relationships (Richards and Richards 1995).

Concluding comments

There is no doubt that new information technologies and the more effective exploitation of visual materials offer a valuable extension to the panoply of methods available to the cross-national qualitative researcher. In part, they assist in the accommodation of chronic problems of language and, in some circumstances, cultural context. Nonetheless, mainstream research enterprise will remain firmly rooted in these two dimensions of national variation and, whilst they constitute a frustrating constraint, they also represent a challenging intellectual opportunity. This is all the more so in the contemporary scientific environment where political and funding aegis demands that a cross-national perspective be routinely incorporated into research design.

Notes

1. Details of the Cross-National Research Group and the associated *Cross-National Research Papers* are available, via the European Research Centre at Loughborough University, on its website at http://info.lboro.ac.uk/departments/eu/cross-national-research.html.
2. Too many of the qualitative methods texts appear to me to be unhelpfully zealous in their dismissal of the quantitative approach to treating social phenomena. Given a specific problematic, sole reliance on qualitative or quantitative analysis could render misleading results, such as attempts to model European welfare regimes by using quantitative indicators that produce a partial explanation. By these criteria, southern states are converging with the north in gross domestic product (GDP) terms

but, this provides little indication of the quality of the welfare system in terms of access, citizenship rights and so forth, since expenditures may be largely driven by demographic and conjunctural factors. The problem then becomes the analytical accommodation of different methods. Although in his classic study of welfare regimes, Esping-Andersen (1990) advocates a productive combination of quantitative and qualitative approaches, his analysis has been criticized for narrow operationalization based on too parsimonious a selection of variables, as well as a systematic bias towards over-reliance on quantification (Cnaan 1992, Lewis 1994).

3. A plethora of literature refers to the cultural boundedness of concepts. Fontana and Frey (1998) report on studies where linguistic competence did not prevent the interviewer from committing social faux pas. Ferguson (1987) reviews the cultural biases in reporting and interpreting the gender division of household roles. Relying on Galtung, Hantrais in this edition refers to the varying intellectual predilections in Europe, although certain disciplines have been more open to international dialogue and collaboration than others. Kinnear (1987) has studied the 'interference' posed by the individual researcher's cultural background in East/West research. Intellectual traditions also carry over into professional practice, as recorded by Ramon (1987) in her study of professional cultures with regard to the practice of psychiatry in Italy and the UK.

4. Nicole-Drancourt (1989) records the problem of interpreting 'life history' in the French context. The nearest equivalent, *trajectoire*, she argues is a more vigorous, temporally-loaded concept. Poverty has been problematic both methodologically (Gardiner 1992) and conceptually (MacGregor 1992). One resolution of these problems is scarcely commendable and involves a form of linguistic imperialism. The term 'gender', for example, translates imperfectly into Latin languages (Letablier 1989), but Anglo-Saxon interpretations have tended to be imposed on the international lexicon.

5. In addition to authors cited here, particularly to be recommended for initiates in comparative methods is the collection of papers edited by Denzin and Lincoln (1998).

References

Bastard, B., Vonèche, C. and Maclean, M. (1989) Women's resources after divorce: Britain and France. *Cross-National Research Papers*, **1**(5), 29–38.

Bendikat, E. (1996) Qualitative historical research on municipal policies. In L. Hantrais and S. Mangen (eds) *Cross-National Research Methods in the Social Sciences* (London: Pinter), pp 129–137.

Bowler, I. (1997) Problems with interviewing: experiences with service providers. In G. Miller and R. Dingwall (eds) *Context and Method in Qualitative Research* (London: Sage), pp 66–76.

Bryman, A. (1988) *Quantity and Quality in Social Research* (London: Unwin Hyman).

Chamberlayne, P. and King, A. (1996) Biographical approaches in comparative work: the 'Cultures of Care' project. In L. Hantrais and S. Mangen (eds) *Cross-National Research Methods in the Social Sciences* (London: Pinter), pp 95–104.

Cicourel, A. (1964) *Method and Measurement in Sociology* (London: Macmillan).

Cnaan, R. A. (1992) Review of 'Three Worlds of Welfare Capitalism'. *Acta Sociologica*, **35**, 69–71.

Coffey, A. and Atkinson, P. (1996) *Making Sense of Qualitative Data* (London: Sage).

Cooper, A., Hetherington, R., Baistow, K., Pitts, J. and Spriggs, A. (1995) *Positive Child Protection: A View from Abroad* (Lyme Regis: Russell House).

Creswell, J. (1998) *Qualitative Inquiry and Research Design: Choosing Among Five Traditions* (London: Sage).

Deacon, B. (1987) The comparative analysis of surveys of opinion about welfare policy in Britain and Hungary. *Cross-National Research Papers*, **1**(4), 15–28.

Denzin, N. K. and Lincoln, Y. S. (1998) *Strategies of Qualitative Inquiry* (London: Sage).

Dogan, M. and Pelassy, D. (1984) *How to Compare Nations: Strategies in Comparative Politics* (First Edition) (London: Chatham House).

Esping-Andersen, G. (1990) *The Three Worlds of Welfare Capitalism* (Cambridge: Polity Press).

Ferguson, M. (1987) New perspectives on male roles. *Cross-National Research Papers*, **1**(3), 51–62.

Fontana, A. and Frey, J. H. (1998) Interviewing: the art of science. In N. K. Denzin and Y. S. Lincoln (eds) *Collecting and Interpreting Qualitative Materials* (London: Sage), pp 47–78.

Gardiner, K. (1992) Measuring poverty comparing low incomes in France and the UK. *Cross-National Research Papers*, **2**(7), 25–36.

Hakim, C. (1987) *Research Design: Strategies and Choices in the Design of Social Research* (London: Unwin Hyman).

Hantrais, L. (1989) Approaches to cross-national comparison. *Cross-National Research Papers*, Special Issue, 9–19.

Hantrais, L. and Ager, D. (1985) The language barrier to effective cross-national research. *Cross-National Research Papers*, **1**(1), 29–40.

Hantrais, L. and Mangen, S. (eds) (1996) *Cross-National Research Methods in the Social Sciences* (London: Pinter).

Harding, A. (1996) Cross-national research and the 'new community power'. In L. Hantrais and S. Mangen (eds) *Cross-National Research Methods in the Social Sciences* (London: Pinter), pp 184–194.

Harkness, J. (1998) *Cross-Cultural Survey Equivalence* (Mannheim: Zentrum für Umfragen, Methoden und Analysen).

Harper, D. (1998) On the authority of the image: visual methods at the crossroads. In N. K. Denzin and Y. S. Lincoln (eds) *Collecting and Interpreting Qualitative Materials* (London: Sage), pp 130–149.

Harwin, J. (1987) Child care in the USSR and England and Wales: some theoretical and practical issues. *Cross-National Research Papers*, **1**(4), 43–56.

Kinnear, R. (1987) Interference from the researcher's background in comparisons across the ideological divide. *Cross-National Research Papers*, **1**(4), 9–14.

Lawrence, P. (1988) In another country. In A. Bryman (ed.) *Doing Research in Organisations* (London: Routledge), pp 96–107.

Le Feuvre, N. (1989) Conceptualising the leisure time of French women. *Cross-National Research Papers*, Special Issue, 56–66.

Leff, J. (1985) The expression of emotion in different cultures: some lessons for cross-national theory and method. *Cross-National Research Papers*, **1**(1), 68–70.

Letablier, M. T. (1989) Women's work and employment in France and Britain; problems of comparability from a French perspective. *Cross-National Research Papers*, Special Issue, 24–33.

Letablier, M. T. and Beechey, V. (1989) Women's work and employment in France and Britain: a cooperative research project. *Cross-National Research Papers*, Special Issue, 89–91.

Lewis, J. (1994) A comment on family policy and the welfare of women in cross-national perspective. *Cross-National Research Papers*, **3**(3), 1–8.

Lisle, E. (1985) Validation in the social sciences by international comparison. *Cross-National Research Papers*, **1**(1), 29–40.

Mabbett, D. and Bolderson, H. (1999) Theories and methods in comparative social policy. In J. Clasen (ed.) *Comparative Social Policy: Concepts, Theories and Methods* (Oxford: Blackwell), pp 34–56.

MacGregor, S. (1992) Poverty, marginalisation and dualism: a commentary. *Cross-National Research Papers*, **2**(7), 1–11.

MacGregor, S. (1993) The semantics and politics of urban poverty. *Cross-National Research Papers*, **3**(2), 65–78.

Mangen, S. (1992) Marginalisation in inner city Europe *Cross-National Research Papers*, **2**(7), 55–72.

Manning, N. (1993) The impact of the EC on social policy at national level: the case of Denmark, France and the UK. *Cross-National Research Papers*, **3**(1), 15–32.

Mason, J. (1996) *Qualitative Researching* (London: Sage).

May, T. (1993) *Social Research: Issues, Methods and Process* (Buckingham: Open University Press).

Miles, M. B. and Huberman, A. M. (1994) *Qualitative Data Analysis: An Expanded Sourcebook* (Second Edition) (London: Sage).

Millar, J. (1990) The socio-economic position of single women in Europe. *Cross-National Research Papers*, **2**(3), 29–41.

Nicole-Drancourt, C. (1989) Conceptual equivalence: female strategies, *trajectoires* and part-time work. *Cross-National Research Papers*, Special Issue, 67–71.

Ramon, S. (1987) The making of a professional culture: professionals in psychiatry in Britain and Italy since 1945. *Cross-National Research Papers*, **1**(3), 35–49.

Richards, T. and Richards, L. (1995) Using hierarchical categories in qualitative data analysis. In U. Kelle (ed.) *Computer Aided Qualitative Data Analysis: Theory, Methods and Practices* (London: Sage), pp 80–95.

Roy, C. (1989) Time-budget methods: towards new concepts for cross-national comparisons. *Cross-National Research Papers*, Special Issue, 72–75.

Sartori, G. (1978) Faulty concepts. In P. G. Lewis, D. C. Potter and F. G. Castles (eds) *The Practice of Comparative Politics: A Reader* (Second Edition) (London: Longman) pp 228–265.

Schunk, M. (1996) Constructing models of the welfare mix: care options of frail elders. In L. Hantrais and S. Mangen (eds) *Cross-National Research Methods in the Social Sciences* (London: Pinter), pp 84–94.

Silverman, D. (1993) *Interpreting Qualitative Data: Methods for Analysing Talk, Text and Interaction* (London: Sage).

Soydan, H. (1996) Using the vignette method in cross-cultural comparisons. In L. Hantrais and S. Mangen (eds) *Cross-National Research Methods in the Social Sciences* (London: Pinter), pp 84–94.

Stanley, L. and Temple, B. (1996) Doing the business: using qualitative software packages in the analysis of qualitative datasets. In R. G. Burgess (ed.) *Using Computers in Qualitative Research* (Greenwich, USA: JAL), pp 169–193.

Stake, R. E. (1998) Case studies. In N. K. Denzin and Y. S. Lincoln (eds) *Strategies of Qualitative Inquiry* (London: Sage), pp 86–109.

Strauss, A. and Corbin, J. (1990) *Basics of Qualitative Research: Grounded Theory Procedures and Techniques* (London: Sage).

Ungerson, C. (1996) Qualitative methods. In L. Hantrais and S. Mangen (eds) *Cross-National Research Methods in the Social Sciences* (London: Pinter), pp 63–65.

van de Vijver, F. and Leung, K. (1997) *Methods and Data Analysis for Cross-Cultural Research* (London: Sage).

Warman, A. and Millar, J. (1996) Researching family obligations: some reflections on methodology. *Cross-National Research Papers*, **4**(4), 23–231.

In pursuit of quality: issues for cross-national survey research

JANET HARKNESS

Introduction

This paper discusses quality issues in quantitative survey research from a cross-national perspective, dealing in particular with issues related to monitoring and evaluating quality. What counts as quality survey research has been defined for the national context over the course of time by the disciplines involved in the survey profession (Groves 1989, Lyberg *et al.* 1997). As used here, the term survey quality is closely related to survey measurement, and monitoring and minimizing survey error (cf., Groves 1989, Biemer *et al.* 1991, Lessler and Kalsbeek 1992, Lyberg *et al.* 1997). It should be understood to include evaluation of strongly quantifiable aspects of quality with consideration of less readily quantifiable factors, such as perceived respondent burden, ethical considerations in conducting research and, for cross-lingual applications, translation, cultural appropriateness, and assessment of these aspects. Decisions about survey quality, whether in the national or cross-national context, are context-dependent: they depend

Janet Harkness is Director of the German section of the International Social Survey Programme (ISSP) at the Center for Survey Research and Methodology (ZUMA), Post Box 122155, Mannheim D-68072, Germany; e-mail: harkness@zuma.de, and co-ordinator of the methodology research groups in the International Social Survey Programme (ISSP). Her research interests are questionnaire development and adaptation for cross-cultural implementations, translation and assessment techniques for questionnaires, and textual analysis. She is editor of and contributor to a recent volume on cross-cultural survey methods research: *Cross-Cultural Survey Equivalence. ZUMA-Nachrichten Spezial*, No. 3 (ZUMA, 1998), and is chief editor of a multiauthored book on cross-national survey research methods now in preparation.

on the adequacy of the study design, process, and outcomes for the purposes to which a study will be put.

In the cross-national context, discussions of quality in terms of cross-national 'error' and 'quality' are rare and the focus has mainly been on manifold aspects of 'comparability' and 'equivalence' (for example, contributions in Vallier 1971, Warwick and Osherson 1973b, Kohn 1989a, Øyen 1990, Inkeles and Sasaki 1996). While these are central to the success and quality of cross-national survey research, it is argued in this paper that comparability and equivalencies are not sufficient. It is evident, for example, that a series of bad studies carried out in comparable fashion with comparable (poor) outputs will not amount to a quality cross-national study. Similarly, whatever counts as good quality in given national contexts may be unrelated to comparability in cross-national terms. What is needed, we suggest, is an interdependent combination of the two: within-country optimizations of across-country objectives, designs, stipulated procedures and required outcomes. We propose that the monitoring, documentation and evaluation procedures now advocated as best practice at national level should be carried over, in modified form, into cross-national research.

Whether the quality of a study can be monitored or evaluated with any confidence depends to a considerable extent on the availability of information about each aspect of the study. Hence, the very considerable concern in the national context with monitoring each stage in survey research (for example, Groves 1989, Biemer et al. 1991, Lessler and Kalsbeek 1992, Lyberg et al. 1997). At the cross-national level, the information needed to be able to monitor or evaluate survey error is largely lacking. Thus, a major step that is necessary for demonstrating quality at the cross-national level involves securing detailed and comparable documentation of cross-national project designs, processes and outcomes.

The absence of information in the cross-national context and the obstacles this poses for quality assessment are a constant theme in what follows. A simple example is that of having access to the questions asked in a survey. Many surveys are designed to have the 'same' questions asked in each country, often as translations from a source questionnaire formulated in English. Countries where English is the native language do not translate, although they do adapt in expected and unexpected fashions. Other countries translate, unless, as occasionally happens, English is used as a *lingua franca* for a survey. However, projects in which different language versions of a questionnaire are used do not always make these publicly available. In research publications, too, questions are frequently discussed without the non-English question wording being presented. The implication in both instances is that the translations 'got it right'. Without access to the texts actually used, however, comparative analysis of data can only be based on 'faith' that the same questions have, indeed, been asked.

Major national and international professional associations have formulated general principles of good practice and rules of ethical conduct, often publicly available on web sites. Examples are the American Association of Public Opinion Research (AAPOR), the British Market Research Quality Standards Association (MRQSA), the German Science Foundation (Kaase 1999), and international organizations such as the

World Association of Public Opinion Research (WAPOR), and the European Society for Opinion and Marketing Research (ESOMAR). In addition to general guidelines, AAPOR has published principles of *Best Practices for Survey and Public Opinion Research* (American Association for Public Opinion Research 1997).

Such principles of best practice provide a framework within which survey quality can be pursued and evaluated. In the absence of a corresponding set of principles specifically tailored for cross-national contexts, we propose to take those of AAPOR as a starting point in raising questions about quality in cross-national surveys. These standards cover core features of research design, process, and the products. They include disclosure controls with procedures and regulations to protect those providing or collecting information, as well as observance of standards of minimal disclosure, that is providing enough information about a study to permit replication and evaluation. The AAPOR best practices consist of the 12 maxims set out below. The details of each are omitted here.

- Have specific goals for the survey;
- Consider alternatives to using a survey to collect information;
- Select samples that will represent the population to be studied;
- Use designs that balance costs with errors;
- Take great care in matching question wording to the concepts being measured and the population studied;
- Pre-test questionnaires and procedures to identify problems prior to the survey;
- Train interviewers carefully on interviewing techniques and the subject matter of the survey;
- Construct quality checks for each stage of the survey;
- Maximise co-operation or response rates within the limits of ethical treatment of human subjects;
- Use statistical analytic and reporting techniques appropriate to the data collected;
- Carefully develop and fulfill pledges of confidentiality given to respondents;
- Disclose all methods of the survey to permit evaluation and replication.

Having suggested that information and documentation are crucial in monitoring quality, we must also emphasize that there are limits to the transparency which documentation can provide, in either national or cross-national contexts. Quite apart from what can be very significant issues of openness—how much detail organizations are prepared or able to reveal about their work—studies documented as having been conducted to the same standards will, nonetheless, produce different qualities of data. This applies at least as much across countries as within countries. Moreover, individual indicators of quality are often both indirect and interdependent on other indicators of quality. Consequently, enhancement of one indicator may have a negative effect on another. In addition, the potential for enhancement of one or the other indicator differs across survey contexts. Response rate improvement is a good example. Extensive and refined refusal conversion techniques (persuading people who do not wish to participate to participate) are more accepted and also more successful in some countries than in others. These countries may, however, also train interviewers more effectively than countries with stricter rules about 'pursuing' sample units. The survey climate, that is public willingness to participate in surveys, may also differ. It is then difficult to separate out the extent to which aggressive pursuit or better communicative skills, or both, contribute to explaining differences in response rates across countries. Moreover, extensive use of recommended procedures to reduce non-response may improve response rates but increase, or at least not reduce, sample bias. Conversely, less than desirable response rates may say little about sample bias (Koch 1998).

Across-country research requirements

Cross-national survey projects compare data collected in different countries or nation states. To warrant comparison, the studies and the data collected must be sufficiently similar or comparable. Studies often aim for comparability of questions by using an 'ask-the-same-questions' design, taking a source questionnaire with questions felt to 'work' everywhere, and adapting this through translation. This is by far the most common approach for reasons not gone into here, and the following discussion relates to surveys using such a model. Nonetheless, it is not the only approach, nor necessarily always the best option. Alternative approaches ask different questions in different cultures which are considered to measure the same construct or dimension (Przeworski and Teune 1970, Triandis and Marin 1983). Even surveys following an 'ask-the-same-questions' model may take a different tack on background information questions. One example are questions to tap religiosity. In many Western countries, a question on the frequency of 'church' attendance can be a suitable indirect measurement of religiosity. It is less suitable, however, for cultures in which religious observance is carried out at an altar at home. Similarly, a question on frequency of prayer or related behaviours might work well as a measure of religiosity for some cultures but not, depending on design, for those in which frequent daily prayer is a requirement.

Leaving aside comparability issues relating to appropriate units, levels and techniques of analysis (see other authors in this volume, and Przeworski and Teune 1970, Verba 1971, contributions in Kohn 1989b, Scheuch 1989), and the core design requirements of equivalence of constructs and of measurement validity and reliability (see also, van de Vijver and Leung 1997), other aspects of studies must also be comparable. These are, briefly, all the other major components of the project: study implementations, processes and products. Apart, perhaps, from sampling, these aspects of cross-national studies–such as defining population frames, deciding modes of administration and fielding procedures, and establishing required data processing and harmonization measures–have been given less attention in comparative literature and study reporting. They raise the question of how to decide what degree of similarity is sufficient for such aspects or, alternatively, how much difference is acceptable.

In concrete, practical terms, cross-national sample surveys are full of differences at each stage of research, ranging from differences in sample sizes and design details, fielding dates and lengths, to differences in regional versus national coverage. South American countries, for example, may cope with fielding difficulties and population distributions by concentrating on sampling urban areas rather than national sampling. There will be differences across countries in item non-response–that is, refusing to answer questions about, for example, income, voting, or sexual behaviour–and response rates will differ depending on factors such as the survey climate in each country. Similarly, different administrative modes (mail, interview or telephone), dictated variously by geography, degree of literacy, telephone coverage or survey budgets, different background variable formulation and coverage, variations in questionnaire content and design, and an array of differences related to language and culture-in-language, are all the rule rather than the exception. Some differences are unavoidable, some may also promote comparability at a deeper level. For instance, seasonal differences across the world mean that if fielding months were (or could be) fixed in a cross-national project, different seasons with different work, vacation, and weather patterns would result. Each of these can, however, affect responses to a variety of topics, from emotional well-being to unemployment rates.

Researchers will disagree on the extent to which certain variations affect comparability. In part, disagreement stems from different theoretical standpoints. In addition, proponents of 'ask-the-same-question' models argue this is the only way to ensure item equivalence and scalar equivalence. Advocates of emic/etic models (Triandis and Marin 1983, de Vera 1985), on the other hand, are among those who argue more for functional equivalence. Disagreements are also related to what is held to be standard and necessary in a given survey community. Some views on standard requirements for comparability are widely held across communities. Many would balk at comparing data from probability samples with data from non-probability samples, the first being widely regarded as the only sample basis suitable for academic sample surveys (but see below). Less consensus is likely on the degree to which certain modes across countries affect the comparability of data. Thus data from a mail survey might be happily compared with data from a face-to-face survey, but more concern would be expressed about comparing data from a telephone survey with data from an interview (contributions in Saris and Kaase 1997).

Meta-information towards a cross-national perspective

Relevant documentation is essential to pursue comparability and other aspects of cross-national quality. However, documentation required for evaluation at the national level is not a ready-made solution for monitoring and evaluation at the cross-national level, since decisions about where to draw dividing lines between acceptable and unacceptable quality need to be made from a cross-national perspective. To acquire such a perspective, meta-information across countries is needed about each survey context, on how studies are usually conducted, but also on how they can be conducted in each country. An understanding is needed, too, of the national parameters for different aspects of the survey process and how these impact in a given country on survey error and quality. This involves articulating and recording information sometimes rarely articulated for the national context. In one context, for example, telephone technology, social structures and related customer habits may make numbers difficult to identify, people hard to reach directly, and householders suspicious of out-of-town calls they are able to identify before answering the telephone. Complicated context considerations such as these find their way into national reporting on telephone sample issues. However, in a country where few or very particular people have a telephone, researchers writing for their national readership are less likely to state that few people have a telephone, since this goes without saying. Not surprisingly, then, much of the material and information needed for such a meta-perspective has not yet been drawn together. The situation may be starting to change: the British Office of National Statistics is preparing to publish a report on aspects of survey practice across Western European countries with the goal of providing meta-information (personal communication, Wim de Heer, Statistics Netherlands; see also Colledge and March 1997).

As envisaged here, a meta-perspective begins with the collection of information concerning different countries. This information would then be assessed in the light of findings from methods research. Naturally enough, in the cross-national context, findings from mono-cultural research need to be supplemented by complementary cross-cultural research. Some of the areas of relevance are, for example, research on communicative principles in different survey contexts, related, for example, to response patterns, response rates and translation; on culturally anchored realizations of social desirability, such as yea-saying, nay-saying, extreme response styles; on adaptation of answer scales related to translation (Mohler et al., 1998) and to social desirability; on visual adaptations for different reading cultures, such as designs from left to right in cultures which read from right to left; and on testing, assessing and pre-testing multiple language designs and implementations. For the most part, however, such cross-cultural methods research is the exception, not the rule.

The sobering truth is that the information available about individual components of cross-national projects is generally well below that required by national standards of best practice, which stipulate sufficient disclosure to allow a study to be replicated and evaluated. Moreover, research publications and study documentation materials suggest that disclosure requirements may frequently be below good practice standards. Thorough-going evaluation of individual data sets, therefore, becomes arduous or impossible. Whatever is lacking for the national level is automatically also unavailable for the cross-national level. Blatantly obvious discrepancies across studies excepted, this leaves the question of comparability unanswered.

Moreover, the detail and specific features recommended in best practice standards for national studies will not always be appropriate for cross-national work. One country's set of standards, no matter how excellent, cannot simply be taken over into cross-national research. If distinctions and categories are to remain common across countries, they automatically become broader, with less and different detail than pertinent for studies within one social and survey context. Nonetheless, the absence of even very basic information makes it impossible in many cases to begin to assess study error and quality. While this is regrettable and undesirable for 'one-off' studies, it is unacceptable for long-term study projects and programmes producing research across countries and across time. Focusing for the moment solely on documentation after the event, that is, once studies have been completed, the most common obstacles can be summarized as:

- Documentation in general and at every level (including the level of data and data editing) is too meagre;
- Information actually collected is not always made publicly available, thus establishing what is actually collected takes on something of the nature of detective work;
- Documentation, if available, is uneven across and within countries;
- Publicly available materials are not tailored for a readership not already 'in the know', for example, secondary analysts;
- Materials (such as questionnaires, background variables, reports) not in English remain more inaccessible than necessary, since notes are rarely inserted in the survey *lingua franca* of English to help people recognize what they might need to read in translation.

Culturally anchored origins of standards

The Anglo-American survey profession has been a major force in defining the basis of what counts as quality in survey research. Standards of best practice are, thus, largely of Western, often originally US, origin. Consequently, they reflect the interest and expense that have gone into improving survey research in certain Western countries, as well as their relevance to the contexts in which they were developed and the potential available there to realize the standards.

Complying with these standards may, obviously, present a challenge for countries with less developed survey traditions and/or radically different social structures. The same holds, however, for countries with highly developed but non-Anglophone survey traditions. In France, for example, probability sampling is less generally used and harder to organize than in a number of neighbouring survey communities. Quota sampling is correspondingly held in greater regard (Deville 1992). In other countries again, social and cultural parameters make it difficult to meet requirements taken for granted elsewhere. In countries without a survey tradition, respondents are not 'survey literate', and there is also a corresponding shortage of experienced fielding institutes. This can present challenges for getting a survey done at all and, certainly, for implementing studies in comparable fashion across a range of countries. In some locations, rules of social interaction require another (insider) person to be present when an outsider (interviewer) speaks to individuals. In multilingual contexts, interviewers may themselves recruit insider or outsider interpreters to translate/ interpret on the spot. In this situation, the interviewers have no real control over what is conveyed to respondents, nor what is conveyed to them about respondents' answers. These two examples illustrate situations that run counter to preferred (Western) good practice. On the one hand, preferred practice is to have interviewers work with respondents without others present, so as to avoid third party influence on responses. On the other, preferred practice requires interviewers to adhere strictly to scripts throughout interviews, which would call for a written translation to be available (see also Houtkoop-Steenstra, in press, on the viability of sticking to scripts).

Perspectives on comparability

The terminology used to refer to different kinds of comparability, as well as the various definitions and distinctions made between different elements vary widely across authors and time. These distinctions cannot be examined here (see equivalence overview in Johnson 1998). In the following, we briefly indicate three perspectives on comparability: requirements that have been emphasized from the early days of cross-national survey research; features emphasized in the 1990s; and, by way of example, requirements set by one survey programme to promote comparability.

Certain aspects have long been seen as key requirements for comparability in cross-national projects. In the words of Warwick and Osherson (1973a: vii), 'the core issue considered is equivalence'. They are referring here to the complex and central issues of equivalence of concepts, equivalence of measurement, linguistic equivalence, as well as sampling equivalence. Also emphasized from an early date are distinctions directed at the appropriateness of what is analysed and how it is analysed, that is, equivalence of levels of research, equivalence of units of analysis, and equivalence of social contexts and appropriate analytical techniques (contributions in Kohn 1989b, Scheuch 1989, Dogan and Pelassy 1990, and see Hantrais in this volume).

Literature in the 1990s documents a predictable continuing interest in the core issues above (contributions in Øyen 1990), concentrated efforts to establish standards and guidelines for translation, and a number of new emphases, briefly outlined below.

Firstly, the pronounced concern for study monitoring and its impact on product quality in the monocultural context has led to an increased interest in these issues at cross-national level, perhaps as researchers meeting requirements in the national context and in their own contributions to cross-national research begin to call for them to be met elsewhere (Park and Jowell 1997, Saris and Kaase 1997, Jowell 1998).

Secondly, the growth in global applications of medical and cognitive testing instruments, for example, has been accompanied by concentrated efforts to establish guidelines for adaptation and translation of instruments. In particular, Hambleton (1994), van de Vijver and Hambleton (1996), Hambleton and Patsula (1998) tackle general guidelines for translation and questionnaire adaptation; Harkness and Schoua-Glusberg (1998) provide a general description for survey translation and appraise various survey translation approaches and assessment procedures. On a more specific topic, Borg (1998) explores connections between underlying referential aspects of questions, facet analysis and translation documentation.

On a different tack, van de Vijver and Leung (1997) and van de Vijver and Tanzer (1999) propose a re-organized scheme of equivalencies and biases in instruments for cross-cultural implementation and discuss how to test questions and data for bias. Saris (1998) and Saris et al., (1998) are recent applications of multitrait-multimethod procedures in predicting and optimizing data quality in cross-national projects. Recent applications of item response theory to detecting item bias across cultures are discussed in van de Vijver and Leung (1997: 72–83).

A further area to receive increased attention has been the lack of comparability in the cross-national context across 'factual' data from official data sources (Hantrais and Letablier 1996, Hantrais and Mangen 1996) and of background variables in survey research (Harkness et al. 1997, Hoffmeyer-Zlotnik and Warner 1998) and marketing research (Bates 1998).

Finally, long-standing concerns about constructs, measurements, translations, and the appropriate selection of data for analysis are increasingly discussed in conjunction with a concern for quality control and study process comparability, and the need to select from the relative wealth of data now available. Svallfors (1996), Jowell (1998), and Küchler (1998) discuss comparability problems in analysing merged data from the International Social Survey Programme (ISSP) programme; and contributions in Saris and Kaase (1997) discuss problems faced in analysing Eurobarometer data across modes.

Regularly conducted cross-national survey programmes are a major source of data across countries and across time. Examples of well-known programmes are the annual ISSP, the European Community Household Panel (ECHP), the less frequent World Values Survey programme, and the biannual (Standard) Eurobarometer, as well as various other 'Barometer', including the Central and Eastern Eurobarometer and the Latinobarometro, conducted in South America. Programme design guidelines and technical reports, if available, indicate the elements viewed as important for comparability. The ISSP Working Principles, the Standard Questions (posted on the web site at http://www.issp.org) and the ISSP National Study Descriptions refer to comparability of sampled population, sample type, the number of cases to be realized, documentation of outcome rates and fielding details, non-ambiguity of source questionnaire questions, equivalence of concepts across countries, minimization of cultural bias, as well as formal equivalence of questions asked across countries and languages.

Pursuing (tracking) quality: the example of translation

The documentation available on translations in surveys illustrates the difficulties met in trying to track, improve or evaluate quality. Generally speaking, documentation for individual studies on how translations are supposed to be undertaken (design stage), are undertaken and assessed (process stages), and the results (outcome stages) are rudimentary at best (Harkness and Schoua-Glusberg 1998). Much of the appropriate documentation would not be difficult to provide. Despite the frequent references to the centrality of language issues in survey literature, the absence of such information suggests that survey translation is perceived as a technical obstacle to be overcome and forgotten, unless 'errors' are picked up. Without documentation for, and on, translation, however, statements about individual translation quality and questionnaire text comparability across countries are unreliable. In order to foster, monitor, evaluate and simply work with instrument translations, something along the following lines of information and documentation is needed. None of what is suggested below is, however, standard practice:

- Source questionnaire annotations for translation (pointers, notes and explanations in the source text to guide primary and secondary researchers and translators). For example, if the item: 'Have you ever taken anything (even a pin or a button) that belonged to someone else?' (Marlowe-Crowne 1960) needs to be translated, a note that these 'buttons' and 'pins' are ornamental and worn in lapels and that the goal is to mention something of little value but of a certain appeal, easily lost and easily picked up, would doubtless facilitate many translations.
- Notes on translated questionnaires for unavoidable differences. A note, for example, that 'ethnic' has deliberately been translated in terms of something approximating 'nationality', or that 'the arts and literature' comes out as something like 'culture' or as 'art and literature' (ISSP 1995 examples) are all useful to researchers interpreting data (Smith and Jarko 1998). Answer scales typically involve unavoidable differences across languages.
- Records of assessment procedures employed, outcomes of these and ensuing steps and consequences, which are important for quality assessment and for working with data.
- Details of problems, differences, or weaknesses found after fielding, to be posted as they become apparent on data web sites and in up-datable electronic code books to help researchers working with data. Currently these are only found in anecdotal form in publications.

One of the few pieces of information reported with some regularity about survey translations is that 'back-translation' was employed. Back-translation is a procedure first advocated for translation assessment for questionnaires in cross-cultural psychology in the 1970s (Brislin 1970, Werner and Campbell 1970). The idea behind back-translation as used for questionnaires is that a text which is itself a translation is translated back into the original language. Differences between the original and the back translation are then used to decide whether the third text (which presumably cannot be read) is a good translation. In practical and theoretical terms (results, effort, costs, reliability, viability), it is one of the less recommendable procedures (Harkness and Schoua-Glusberg 1998). Ironically, the problem is that, if a study description states that a back-translation was carried out (as in Eurobarometer reports), this will be read by many as an indicator of quality. Conversely, if countries report they did not carry out back-translations, this may be interpreted as a lack of quality (as in Park and Jowell 1997).

Obstacles to improving the quality of cross-national survey research

Since the early days, the names of researchers well-known in cross-national research have read like a Who's Who in empirical research. However, the funding situation for comparative research is less healthy. Finding funds for academic comparative research is often difficult at anything above the two-country level. Securing funding for methods research across numerous countries is considerably more difficult. Those involved in comparative methods research are, consequently, researchers centrally interested in analysing the data; their methodological interests are understandably driven by the need to come to terms with data, studies or documentation causing problems. The emphasis in literature on comparative research thus automatically falls on what can go wrong, on inadequacies, errors and problems. Finding solutions for problems must certainly take priority. At the same time, it can mean that methods research is re-active rather than pro-active and that efforts are restricted to one particular problem in one particular backyard. More general perspectives, cross-disciplinary initiatives and sustained large-scale co-operation on methodological issues are, for obvious reasons, rare.

The frequently re-iterated standpoint that there is nothing essentially different about doing cross-national research (see other authors in this volume) may wrongly be taken as also conveying that a detailed methodology for cross-national research is also already available, and all that researchers now need to do is analyse appropriately and, perhaps, set up quality monitoring procedures. The view taken here, however, is that a calibrated methodology for cross-cultural survey research is not yet available. What we do have are increasingly sophisticated methods and detailed findings for national contexts. These are of central importance for cross-national research. At the same time, they cannot simply be applied as they stand in cross-national contexts. Research, like anything else a society produces, is culture bound. As a result, methodological elaborations are now needed which allow available, often sophisticated, methods to be applied successfully and appropriately across countries (cross-cultural bridges, transformations, and innovations). Without greater acknowledgement of the need for methodological refinement for cross-national, cross-cultural applications, accompanied by changes in funding policies, progress on the comparative methods front has little chance of keeping up with the rapidly expanding investment in decision-making and policy planning on the basis of globally collected but potentially questionable data.

Comparability can only be based on degrees of similarity, which automatically requires that we can establish ranges, if not points, for cut-offs. To set these realistically and in advance, we need to be clear about the degree to which participants are able to comply with requirements and the extent to which alternative options are acceptable. Deep procedural definition of requirements can be helpful. Thus, if the population from which the sample in each country should be drawn is initially defined as the 'adult population in private accommodation', this must be further specified. The actual age range intended (lower and any upper cut-offs), the definition of 'private accommodation' and of 'population' (inhabitants or citizens, both also defined) must each be clarified. Policy decisions are also necessary on the inevitable deviations from definitions. If, for example, in one country no-one over 79 is interviewed, in another no foreigners are interviewed, while another includes people living in accommodation units that are excluded or do not exist elsewhere (trailers or varieties of sheltered accommodation), this affects the comparability of the populations from which samples are drawn. If the effects of differences are negligible, they can be disregarded. However, the effects need to be known and investigated to decide whether they are negligible or not.

If a full probability random sample is the project requirement, some countries may be unable to comply. One option is to bar such countries from joining the project. Another is to include them and accept that researchers may well choose not to analyse data from different kinds of samples. If a single country is the odd country out, this can result in a situation comparable to that of the slow, fat child when the sports team is being picked. The quandary then is both who will use the data from the country with the non-probability sample and which data this country will feel good about comparing with its own. In a world increasingly based on global information, with players' standing and team selection strongly determined by the richness and speed of their access to information, these issues also raise a number of new ethical questions for academic survey research.

Data access and data quality are areas where those carrying out comparative research, those archiving and distributing data, and these using the data must each break new ground. As access to data becomes easier and cheaper, more users of data can potentially result in either more critical or more satisfied users. Researchers are, or ought to be, under pressure to demonstrate the suitability of the data used for the purpose at hand. Publications based on good and user-friendly data can help enhance a project or programme's profile. These, in turn, can help the project find further funding. In the past, researchers carrying out comparative research may well have been resigned to toiling along with unwieldy data sets, piecemeal information and cryptic code books. As more researchers become involved in comparative research, increasingly from a generation accustomed to more user-oriented support, changes are needed to the parameters of what counts as reasonable to deliver and to demand. Articles posted on web sites, for example, can now be linked up to data sets to allow 'readers' to run their own analyses, much in the way software and analysis textbooks are now written to be used with data available on web sites.

Finally, there is a need for critical and open discussion of methods and practices in cross-national research. Recent developments in the ISSP illustrate this point well. It is fairly easy to find out a reasonable amount about the ISSP directly from its web site. Even more can be found out by working with the data, questionnaires and code books. Nonethelesss, it took a number of years and several rounds of self-investigation for the ISSP to discover that it did not like what it was finding out about itself (Svallfors 1996, Park and Jowell 1997, Jowell 1998, Küchler 1998; all are authors who are, or were formerly, active in the ISSP). Officially, many quality requirements were in place from the start. In practice, time lags in data access, the absence of loud complaints among colleagues, and a policy of trust rather than self-policing have meant that covert differences went unnoticed. This is not altogether surprising if we consider that documents in all the ISSP languages had to be checked in order to find certain differences (Harkness 1999). Others were noticed and criticized, but no real 'penalties' were introduced. Others again (such as demographic comparability) have proved resistant to various attempts at improvement. In this connection, we note that the need for proper 'policing' (Jowell 1998) has been neglected in cross-national survey programme management. Even accepting that pressures against openness are at least as strong as those to document and demonstrate quality, and that national constraints on openness set limits to monitoring in the cross-national context, there is very clearly room for improving comparability and quality monitoring. Here, again, the question of funding policies for interdisciplinary, international work becomes salient.

What is surprising, we suggest, is that the ISSP seems to be one of the few projects actively and publicly involved in a methods discourse. For the programme, the benefits of open discussion are apparent. Unhappy with the results of its own self-evaluation (Park and Jowell 1997), the group initiated a process of re-definition and re-iteration of existing principles and of monitoring performance. By 1999, it had authorized extensive new compulsory disclosure and controlling measures.

Pursuit and quest: thinking globally and acting locally

At the local/national level, survey research has never been better equipped to pursue quality research and the potential to act—to carry out demonstrably good research—is given in many survey contexts. At the cross-national level, too, the potential has never been greater to move towards a situation where we have demonstrably comparable, quality data. But the topography of cross-national survey contexts is still only sketchy. Our grasp of a global or meta-perspective on cross-national research is thus rather fragile. As indicated above, an important first step towards gaining this perspective will be the collection of meta-documentation to be used in guiding the development of standards and requirements, and in focusing cross-cultural survey methods research. The Centre for Survey Research and Methodology (ZUMA) in Mannheim, Germany, is in the process of setting up a web site home page to help draw this material together.

Global thinking is needed, in fact, in a number of senses. In order to arrive at a methodology for cross-national studies and for cross-cultural research within multicultural societies, we need to look beyond not only our own national survey standards but also our own networks, fields, and individual expertise. For instance, research being pursued in cross-cultural psychology and in the field of cognitive testing is of direct relevance to cross-national survey research. Research underway in translation studies on translation and translation assessment is highly pertinent for instrument translation. In addition, cognitive psychology has produced a range of findings for survey research still to be worked through from cross-cultural perspectives. Communication theory, linguistics, and text analysis research are each of relevance for developing questionnaire and interviewer materials across countries. In arguing that everything we basically need to conduct cross-national survey research was already available, Scheuch (1989) urged researchers not to re-invent the comparative wheel. For our part, while appreciative of the wealth of research already available, we do feel that some re-engineering is called for and, for the cross-country terrain which cross-national research often involves, we heartily welcome the invention of run-flat tyres.

References

American Association for Public Opinion Research (AAPOR) (1997) *Best Practices for Survey and Public Opinion Research and Survey Practices that AAPOR Condemns* (http://www.aapor.org/best/index.html).

Bates, B.A. (1998) Standard demographic classification. In C. McDonald and P. Vangelder (eds) *ESOMAR Handbook of Market and Opinion Research* (Fourth Edition) (Amsterdam: ESOMAR), pp 105–130.

Biemer, P., Groves, R., Lyberg, L., Mathiowetz, N., and Sudman S. (eds) (1991) *Measurement Error in Surveys*. (New York: John Wiley and Sons).

Borg, I. (1998) A facet-theoretical approach to item equivalency. In J. Harkness (ed.) *Cross-Cultural Survey Equivalence. ZUMA-Nachrichten Spezial*, No. 3 (Mannheim: Zentrum für Umfragen, Methoden und Analysen), pp 145–158.

Brislin, R.W. (1970) Back-Translation for Cross-Cultural Research. *Journal of Cross-Cultural Psychology*, **1**, 185–216.

Colledge, M. and March, M. (1997) Quality, policies, standards, guidelines, and recommended practices at national statistical agencies. In L. Lyberg, P. Biemer, M. Collins, E. de Leeuw, C. Dippo, N. Schwarz and D. Trewin (eds) *Survey Measurement and Process Quality* (New York: John Wiley and Sons), pp 501–522.

Deville, J.-C. (1992) Eléments pour une théorie des enquêtes par quotas. In L Lebart (ed.) *La qualité de l'information dans les enquêtes* (Paris: Dunod), pp 345–364.

Dogan, M. and Pelassy, D. (1990) *How to Compare Nations. Strategies in Comparative Politics* (Second Edition) (Chatham, New Jersey: Chatham House Publishers).

Groves, R. (1989) *Survey Errors and Survey Costs* (New York: John Wiley and Sons).

Hambleton, R.K. (1994) Guidelines for adapting educational and psychological tests: a progress report. *European Journal of Psychological Assessment (Bulletin of the International Test Commission)*, **10**, 229–244.

Hambleton, R.K. and Patsula, L. (1998) Adapting tests for use in multiple languages and cultures. *Social Indicators Research. An International and Interdisciplinary Journal for Quality-of-life Measurement*, **45**(1–3), 153–171.

Hantrais, L. and Letablier, M.-T. (1996) *Families and Family Policies in Europe* (London and New York: Longman).

Hantrais, L. and Mangen, S. (eds) (1996) *Cross-national Research Methods in the Social Sciences* (London: Pinter).

Harkness, J.A. (1999) Report presented to the ISSP General Assembly on translations across ISSP questionnaires. May, Madrid (http://www.issp.org/info.htm#Methodological Research).

Harkness, J.A., Mohler, P.Ph. and McCabe, B. (1997) Towards a manual of European background variables. ZUMA report on background variables in a comparative perspective. In J.A. Harkness, P.Ph. Mohler and R. Thomas (eds) *General Report on Study Programme for Quantitative Research (SPQR)*. Report to the European Commission (Mannheim: ZUMA, mimeo).

Harkness, J.A. and Schoua-Glusberg, A. (1998) Questionnaires in translation. In J.A. Harkness (ed.) *Cross-Cultural Survey Equivalence. ZUMA-Nachrichten Spezial*, No. 3 (Mannheim: Zentrum für Umfragen, Methoden und Analysen), pp 87–128.

Hoffmeyer-Zlotnik, J.H.P. and Warner, U. (1998) Die Messung von Einkommen im nationalen und internationalen Vergleich. *ZUMA–Nachrichten* (Mannheim: Zentrum für Umfragen, Methoden und Analysen), **42**, 30–65.

Houtkoop-Steenstra, H. (in press) *Interaction and the Standardized Survey Interview: The Living Questionnaire* (Cambridge: Cambridge University Press).

Inkeles, A and Sasaki, M. (1996) *Comparing Nations and Cultures* (Englewood Cliffs, New Jersey: Prentice-Hall).

Johnson, T.P. (1998) Approaches to equivalence in cross-cultural and cross-national survey research. In Harkness, J. (ed.) *Cross-Cultural Survey Equivalence. ZUMA-Nachrichten Spezial*, No. 3 (Mannheim: Zentrum für Umfragen, Methoden und Analysen), pp 159–185.

Jowell, R. (1998) How comparative is comparative research? *American Behavioral Scientist*, **42**(2), 168–177.

Kaase, M. (ed.) (1999) *Qualitätskriterien der Umfrageforschung*. Deutsche Forschungsgemeinschaft. Denkschrift (Berlin: Akademie Verlag).

Koch, A. (1998) Wenn 'mehr' nicht gleichbedeutend mit 'besser' ist: Ausschöpfungsquoten und Stichprobenverzerrungen in allgemeinen Bevölkerungsumfragen. ZUMA-Nachrichten (Mannheim: Zentrum für Umfragen, Methoden und Analysen), **42**, 66–90.

Kohn, M.L. (1989a) Cross-national research as an analytic strategy. In M.L. Kohn (ed.) *Cross-National Research in Sociology* (Newbury Park: Sage), pp 77–103.

Kohn, M.L. (ed.) (1989b) *Cross-National Research in Sociology* (Newbury Park: Sage).

Küchler, M. (1998) The survey method: an indispensable tool for social science research everywhere? *American Behavioral Scientist*, **42**(2), 178–200.

Lessler, J. and Kalsbeek W. (1992) *Nonsampling Error in Surveys* (New York: John Wiley and Sons).

Lyberg, L., Biemer, P., Collins, M., de Leeuw, E., Dippo, C., Schwarz, N. and Trewin, D. (eds) (1997) *Survey Measurement and Process Quality* (New York: John Wiley and Sons).

Marlowe, D. and Crowne, D.P. (1960) A new scale of social desirability independent of psychopathology. *Journal of Consulting Psychology*, **24**, 349–354.

Mohler, P.Ph., Smith, T.W. and Harkness, J.A. (1998) Respondents' ratings of expressions from response scales: a two-country, two-language investigation of equivalence and translation. In J.A. Harkness (ed.) *Cross-Cultural Survey Equivalence. ZUMA-Nachrichten Spezial* No. 3 (Mannheim: Zentrum für Umfragen, Methoden und Analysen), pp 159–185.

Øyen, E. (1990) *Comparative Methodology. Theory and Practice in International Social Research* (London: Sage).

Park, A. and Jowell, R. (1997) Consistencies and differences in a cross-national survey. The International Social Survey Programme (1995) (http://www.za.uni-koeln.de/data/en/issp/cdbk_pdf.htm).

Przeworski, A. and Teune, H. (1970) *The Logic of Comparative Social Inquiry* (New York: John Wiley and Sons).

Saris, W.E. (1998) The effects of measurement error in cross-cultural research. In J.A. Harkness (ed.) *Cross-Cultural Survey Equivalence*. *ZUMA-Nachrichten Spezial*, No. 3 (Mannheim: Zentrum für Umfragen, Methoden und Analysen), pp. 67–86.

Saris, W.E. and Kaase, M. (eds) (1997) *EUROBAROMETER Measurement Instruments for Opinions in Europe*. *ZUMA-Nachrichten Spezial*, No. 2 (Mannheim: Zentrum für Umfragen, Methoden und Analysen).

Saris, W.E., van Wijk, T., and Scherpenzeel , A. (1998) Validity and reliability of subjective social indicators. *Social Indicators Research*, **45**, 173–199.

Smith, T.W. and Jarko, L. (1998) National pride: a cross-national analysis. *GSS Cross-National Report*, No. 19 (Chicago: University of Chicago).

Scheuch, E.K. (1989) Theoretical implications of comparative survey research: why the wheel of cross-cultural methodology keeps on being reinvented. *International Sociology*, **4**, 147–167.

Svallfors, S. (1996) National differences in national identities. An introduction to the International Social Survey Programme. *New Community*, **22**, 127–134.

Triandis, H.C. and Marin, G. (1983) Etic plus emic versus pseudoetic: a test of a basic assumption of contemporary cross-cultural psychology. *Journal of Cross-Cultural Psychology*, **14**, 489–500.

van de Vijver, F.J.R. and Hambelton, R.K. (1996) Translating tests: some practical guidelines. In *European Psychologist*, **1**(2), 89–99.

van de Vijver, F.J.R. and Leung, K. (1997) *Methods and Data Analysis for Cross-Cultural Research* (Thousand Oaks, C.A.: Sage).

van de Vijver, F.J.R. and Tanzer, N. (1999) Bias and equivalence in cross-cultural assessment: an overview. *European Review of Applied Psychology*, **41**(4), 263–279.

Vallier, I. (ed.) (1971) *Comparative Methods in Sociology*. *Essays on Trends and Applications* (Berkeley: University of California Press).

Vera de, M.V. (1985) *Establishing Cultural Relevance and Measurement Equivalence using Emic and Etic Items*. Unpublished dissertation (Urbana, IL: University of Illinois).

Verba, S. (1971) Cross-national survey research: the problem of credibility. In I. Vallier (ed.) *Comparative Methods in Sociology*. *Essays on Trends and Applications* (Berkeley: University of California Press), pp 309–353.

Warwick, D. and Osherson, S (1973a) Introduction. In D. Warwick and S. Osherson (eds) *Comparative Research Methods* (Englewood Cliffs, New Jersey: Prentice-Hall, Inc.), pp vi–viii.

Warwick, D. and Osherson, S. (eds) (1973b) *Comparative Research Methods* (Englewood Cliffs, New Jersey: Prentice-Hall, Inc.).

Werner, O. and Campbell, D. (1970) Translating, working through interpreters and the problem of decentering. In R. Naroll and R. Cohen (eds) *American Handbook of Methods in Cultural Anthropology* (New York: National History Press), pp 398–420.

Concepts, context and discourse in a comparative case study

EMMA CARMEL

Introduction

This paper examines the methodological issues arising from the application of critical discourse analysis in a comparative case study. The research aimed to understand how discourses shaped and legitimized policy change and continuity in Germany before and after unification. As a result, two objectives were identified for the research: one empirical and the other theoretical. The policy areas examined were family and labour market policies. The consequent empirical objective was to identify the different ways in which appropriate roles for state, market and family were conceptualized in political and policy discussions and outputs over time. The theoretical aim was to delineate and explain the relationship between policy, politics and discourses in a particular time and place.

By examining the process of unification of two states over time, the importance of comparing changing contexts – political, social and economic – became apparent. The need arose to develop a methodologically defensible, and practically feasible, research strategy for identifying contexts that were directly related to the detailed textual analysis.

Emma Carmel is lecturer in the Department of Social and Policy Sciences, University of Bath, Claverton Down, Bath BA2 7AY, UK. Her research interests cover gender, nationhood and citizenship, comparative policy analysis, legitimation and symbolic power, and the political economy of welfare. This paper is derived from her DPhil thesis, entitled: The Politics of Welfare in the Nation State: Gender, Family and Employment in Germany 1987–1998 (University of York, 1999).

The research strategy involved the analysis of political party and parliamentary documents relating to the two largest parties in Germany: the Christian Democratic Party and the Social Democratic Party, over a ten-year period. This textual analysis was then integrated with a contextual analysis of the institutional and socio-economic framework within which discourses were articulated. The paper offers a critique of the four stages of analysis used in the research: contextual analysis and its relationship to the development of concepts in the study; initial data analysis using computer software; the reassessment of context and discourse; and the integration of theory, context and discourse analysis in writing up the research. The discussion outlines the reasoning behind the strategy and evaluates its methodological and practical consequences for the research.

Case studies and concepts

The research questions in the study focused on a concrete situation, delineated in terms of time and space, which as a singular example of social change is worthy of study in itself (Dogan and Pelassey 1990, Bradshaw and Wallace 1991: 155–157). The aim was to identify the ways in which state, market and family were conceptualized in German policy-making before and after unification. In addition, a case study offered the opportunity to conduct an in-depth examination of differences within Germany (Amenta 1991: 173–174). It allowed for the explicit exploration of inner-German differences in the symbolic construction of policy issues, whether in terms of region such as north/south, as well as the more obvious east/west, political affiliation, gender or citizenship status.

However, methodological difficulties with the role of theory arise in two broad areas of qualitative cross-national research, especially with regard to case studies. The first is a matter of principle: what role can and should theory have? The second is a matter of practice: how might concepts be applied?

Single-country studies aiming to make a theoretical contribution face the criticism that, in being only implicitly comparative (and sometimes not even that), they do not allow theoretical generalizations, or even theoretical conclusions, to be drawn (Kohn 1989, Nowak 1989: 37–39, Keman 1993: 54). Even qualitative researchers fall prey to the positivist emphasis on testing and generalizing theory. Skocpol (1984: 369–374) distinguishes between 'interpretive' and 'analytic' approaches to historical comparative research, where the former is concerned with understanding events and processes, and the latter with explaining their causal regularity. Skocpol argues that the interpretive approach suffers from a concern with detail and depth, and is unable to offer explanatory theories, which can, nonetheless, be developed within the analytic approach. She argues that theoretically rigorous explanations can only be developed through comparative research which identifies a series of necessary and sufficient causes for a particular event. Alternatively, Ragin (1987) adopts Boolean techniques to simplify, and thus make transferable, theoretical explanations of common events while apparently relating them to particular contexts. This was an attempt to combine the theoretical rigour of large-scale studies with the sensitivity to context of small-N studies.

These approaches appear to be seduced by the chimera of objectivity, rigour and generalizability. Both set up a false dichotomy between contextualization and conceptualization in research, which they then 'overcome' by adopting their particular favoured techniques. Skocpol separates 'understanding' from 'explanation', when one actually presupposes the other. While Ragin (1989: 69–70) admires some aspects of the 'qualitative' or small-N approach, the implication of his method is that regular qualitative research can only describe, as it cannot explain, particular phenomena. And this is even translated into claims of greater 'rigour' for Boolean techniques (Griffen et al. 1991: 124–131, Wickham-Crowley 1991: 86–87).

In themselves, both the techniques are useful, and can lead to illuminating, even groundbreaking conceptual insights. However, Ragin and Skocpol deal with 'causally focused' research objectives, where the aim was to establish a particular set of variables to explain a singular event. In research that aims to delineate and explain a series of social relationships, as in the present case, an alternative view of the role of theory might be applied. As the methodological premise of most qualitative research is to develop theoretical perspectives from the particular and the concrete, then theoretical validity should be open primarily to the test of applicability, rather than that of generalizability.

Small-N studies can benefit from the engagement with different contexts, which facilitates the conceptualization of core common features of a particular process, experience or event, without any loss of rigour (Rueschemeyer 1991: 32). One of the advantages of qualitative cross-national research is that the development of such conceptualizations is deeply embedded in the context from which they arose, and thus is concretely linked to particular times and places (Ragin 1989: 69–70, Bradshaw and Wallace 1991: 162). Indeed, the exploratory nature of the present theoretical approach also lent itself to a case study. Before the research commenced, a bundle of possible conceptualizations of symbolic power, discourse, and their possible role in policy-making had been identified. The aim was to work these ideas through the data analysis to refine them, or to examine if a reconceptualization was required. While it is more usual to test existing theories in single-country studies (Amenta 1991: 173–174), the development of a finely honed theoretical framework, or conceptualization of an issue is equally well suited to cross-national case study research (Griffin et al. 1991: 112).

Nonetheless, regarding the practical development and application of concepts, additional issues arise. The development of concepts is complex, requiring imagination and sensitivity in qualitative research in general, and more particularly if a grounded theory or an exploratory approach is taken. In cross-national research, these difficulties are often compounded by the 'non-translatability' or non-transferability of concepts. Both of these have been discussed elsewhere (Pitrou 1994, Jobert 1996, Rainbird 1996, Hantrais in this volume), and it only needs to be emphasized here that linguistic and conceptual clarity is of crucial importance to the qualitative comparativist. It is particularly important if a balance is to be struck between adopting concepts which 'travel' (Rose 1991), and avoiding 'conceptual straining' (Sartori 1973: 184), whereby concepts become so general as to be impossible to apply. Qualitative research has the potential to explore the varying meanings of concepts in different national contexts as part of its comparison. Indeed, using empirical research to break down the concept of care, law, or welfare and to explore the meaning of its (different) components in different locations has theoretical and empirical value in itself (Ferrari 1990: 75).

Contexts and concepts

In comparing the two German states prior to unification, and in providing a context to the documentary analysis which focused on the post-unification state, no attempt at 'functional equivalence' was made. To have done so would have blurred the striking differences between the states which shaped the process of unification after 1990 (Teune 1990: 54). It was precisely by marking out the theoretical and empirical differences between the political, economic and social structures of the states, that post-unification developments in both parts of the country could be analysed.

The first context to be examined was that of the politics and policy-making in both Germanies. Conducted through a conventional literature review and from previous research, the two German polities were 'segmented' (Dogan and Pelassey 1990) according to four features of their political systems. In this case, the constitutions, the structure of political parties, policy-making procedures, and central-local relations in the two states were compared. Additional analysis was undertaken on national and *Land* electoral results (pre-1990 for West Germany only) over the ten-year period. The latter were designed to clarify the political context to policy debates. A three-way scheme was adopted to identify the politico-economic context to the study. The 'free' market was contrasted with the command economy; corporatism with the co-option of trade unions; and the 'social market economy' with the 'unity of economic and social policy'. Secondary data on family composition, as well as employment and unemployment rates were analysed, in order to compare trends in East and West Germany over time, as well as to identify gender differences in each region. Policy expenditures, such as those relating to active and passive labour market policies, and also the profile of active labour market scheme participants were analysed, providing a context of policy outcomes over the period. The latter was designed to assist in the identification of any disjuncture between policy and political discourses, and their respective policy outputs.

Concepts were explored and challenged in two ways in the research. The first related to the theoretical concerns. The detailed analysis of documents revealed that the impact and role of particular constructions could be separated into three types of discourse. Thus, in meeting the theoretical aim of the research, the 'strained concept' of discourse was interrogated and broken down into three types, each of which had a different relationship with politics and policy-making in Germany at this time. The second way was by making concepts such as family, employment, market and state the subject of research, a task for which the techniques of critical discourse analysis were eminently suited. By comparing the meanings conveyed in such concepts between parties, and between East and West German politicians and political groups over time, the analysis facilitated an insight into the political weight and meaning attached to these concepts.

Initial data analysis

The fieldwork was conducted over a period of nine months in Germany, time which was also used to access supplementary German literature on the policy area. In addition to documentary analysis, 'information' interviews were conducted with members of parties, to assist in contextualising the discourse analysis.

Data analysis began in earnest after the end of the fieldwork. This was unsatisfactory for two reasons. The first is that a single visit (if long) did not allow the researcher to 'go back and check' on finer details, although long experience of documentary research meant that the need to do this only arose on one or two occasions. More significantly, the process of analysis required a mental shift back to the context of the country being studied, whereas discussion with colleagues and friends, and daily immersion in the culture and politics during fieldwork had prompted many of the most useful insights into the data. The complexities of the insider/outsider relationship have been little discussed in the literature on cross-national research, and unfortunately there is no space to discuss them here. Important exceptions include Soydan (1996), who argues that an intimate knowledge of the countries being studied is essential, and Chamberlayne and King (1996), who suggest that access to a combination of insider and outsider understandings of the subject and countries may produce the most useful insights into data. Suffice it to say that, even in a study which used data already at two removes from the researcher (as a non-national or resident, and using data produced for other purposes), an intimate knowledge of the countries being studied was invaluable. This was much more difficult, although not impossible, to recapture following departure from Germany. Both these practical difficulties were partially addressed by use of the Internet, newspapers, and continuing e-mail discussions with colleagues, as well as the presence of a trusty research diary.

Notwithstanding the difficulties of distance and outsidership, coding was facilitated by the use of computer software. Faced with six box files of documents from which to elicit changes, over a ten-year period, on two related policy areas from two parties, and their affiliated groups, the software made the exercise of coding infinitely more practicable. Coding was both descriptive (source, date, type of document) and analytical, and was conducted prior to translation.

The program used was NUD*IST (version 4), which, like other qualitative data analysis programmes, is not ideally suited to documentary analysis, although it does make limited provision for it. Each document was skim-read to identify the appropriate division into sections, and these sections were numbered on the document itself to ensure a seamless reference system between the coding and the original document. The coding system was developed according to the ways in which relevant concepts, ideas, policies and events were articulated. Broad subject codes (for example 'state-market relations', or 'employment') acted as titles, or subject headings which subsumed the analytic codes relating to these themes.

The analytic codes were subdivided (and sometimes moved and merged) in order to identify the different ways in which they were discussed and constructed. Thus, under 'employment', one code on deregulation of working time might be justified by the need for labour market flexibility, and another for the same deregulation by the need to facilitate the reconciliation of work and family life.

The hierarchical tree structure of the program created some difficulties in analysis, as did the coding of documents that were external to (i.e. not loaded into and an integral part of) the programme. One of the advantages of computer software is the automatic updating of existing coding in texts when codes are separated or merged. As the documents were not loaded within the programme, this was not possible for the research in hand. Whenever a code was altered, the document sections already coded had to be re-examined to ascertain if the new code was appropriate. This laborious process led to a rather less 'playful' approach to coding than might, otherwise, have been the case. Indeed, the significance of a particular construction might only become clear when it appeared in several documents, which would again entail a return to the documents in order to recode them according to the adjusted codes. This constraint resulted in a tactical decision to reduce the load of coding work by limiting the types of document to be coded. The implications of this decision for consequent analysis are difficult to assess, although a survey of remaining types of document did not indicate any major coding omissions.

Contextualising the analysis

The software was particularly useful in returning to the contextualization of the research. The search tools of the programme facilitated an analysis not only of common or unusual combinations of codes, but also of change over time and the assessment of the different impacts of institutional and socio-demographic factors. In addition, it was possible to identify those constructions of policy problems and solutions that were disputed within and between the parties. In terms of the comparison, the software tools made document sections or particular constructions that focused on East Germany only, or which were articulated by actors or groups associated with the former GDR, readily identifiable. Very few focused on West Germany as a separate entity, which was developed into a minor research finding of itself. By coding document types, it was also possible to assess how different audiences (internal to the party, to particular constituencies, or to an international audience) affected the articulation of discourses. The numerous and straightforward mechanisms for searching the coding in the software facilitated the identification of unusual party documents and times of debates within the parties. The mass of data was transformed into a tractable object of interrogation, as the software provided easy access to overarching patterns (and vital exceptions to them) in data relating to the East/West comparison as well as to the comparison over time (Seidel 1991: 114). The 'playfulness' and experimentation with data, missing from the second stage of the research, returned. 'Memos' on the coding facilitated reflections on the relationship of context and data (Richards and Richards 1991: 45–46), as well as 'auditing' the coding itself, which proved crucial in keeping track of the data and its conceptualization at different stages of the project (Fielding and Lee 1998: 104–106).

As a result, the structure of the contextual analysis was altered. The structures of political parties were analysed with central/local relations, and legislative procedures were considered in conjunction with the place of the constitution. This not only sharpened the focus of the analysis, but also assisted in making sense of the data and understanding the transformation of politics and policies in both East and West Germany.

The second advantage of the flexibility of software was in developing theoretical ideas, offering 'fluidity of text indexing and lightness in exploration of growing theory, and the facility to move between conceptual exploration and the words it is about' (Richards and Richards 1991: 52). The process of analysing changing constructions revealed a series of relationships between different types of discourses, politics and policy-making, which were constantly tested against one another, with new codes being developed by searches which looked for particular patterns in the data.

Integrating theory, context and discourse

As a result of the recontextualization of the research, a multilayered schema of contexts and analysis could be formulated, representing a response to the theoretical and the empirical aims of the research. The aim when writing up the research was to make explicit the process of contextualization as an integral part of the empirical and theoretical analysis.

The analysis of the constitutional contexts (political and economic) was combined with analysis of one of the identified types of discourse, which itself acted as a context to the other types. Conceptually identified as 'consensus structural' discourses, they were shared between the two parties, and were central to the construction of the united Germany's political and economic regime as distinctly West German. The opposing elements associated with the identity of either party, or stream within a party, were identified as 'competitive structural' discourses. This procedure illustrated the theoretical argument, indicating the presence, and interaction, of institutional and discursive contexts to policy debates and outputs. Thus, two types of discourse could be conceptualized as contexts themselves, interacting with the conventional institutional and socio-economic contexts to form a backdrop against which policies were debated and formulated. Having established these interacting contexts in a broad-brush way, the study then went on to present the interaction of these discursive and institutional contexts with policy-making in more fine-grained detail. This procedure fleshed out the theoretical framework derived from the analysis, facilitated by the move from the general (institutional) context, to the detail of the discourse analysis (the two types of 'structural' discourse), to the interaction of both in the production of policy debates and outputs over time.

The process of writing-up required above-average effort in order to capture the complexity of the relationships being examined, while not drowning the analysis in an artificially complicated structure. Yet, despite the extra effort it entailed, it appears warranted, insofar as the methodological premises of the case study required a transparent integration of theory, context and analysis.

Concluding reflections

In evaluating the research strategy for this study, the lessons learned can be divided into the practical and the methodological. Regarding the use of software, there is no doubt that, as a tool for the researcher, it was useful, although care is needed to assess why and how it will add to, or ease, analysis. 'Leaping in' is most likely to lead to uphelpful coding, and reams of computer printout that mean nothing. The contextualization and theorization of the analysis relied on careful and thorough initial coding, and judicious analytical use of the software's tireless searches, not to mention numerous scrawled diagrams and pictures. Nonetheless, adopted as a tool for analysis, it elicited a more reliable view of all the data than could have been achieved with paper and pen alone, and was particularly useful for making consistent comparison of data. Regarding the fieldwork, it is clear that consideration needs to be given to insider/outsider relationships in qualitative comparative research, and that comparative documentary research is much enriched by interviews and an intimacy with the language and social, political and economic environment of the countries being studied.

In terms of methodological issues, it is to be hoped that this case study may stand as a small testament to the possibility for theoretical development based on single-country studies, and also for the value of explicitly analysing context as part of both the theoretical and empirical analysis in comparative qualitative studies.

Acknowledgement

The research discussed in this paper was funded by the Economic and Social Research Council, research grant number R00429534053. Their support is gratefully acknowledged.

References

Amenta, E. (1991) Making the most of a case study: theories of the welfare state and the American experience. In C. Ragin (ed.) *Issues and Alternatives in Comparative Social Research* (Leiden: Brill), pp 172–193.

Bradshaw, Y. and Wallace, M. (1991) Informing generality and explaining uniqueness: the place of case studies in comparative research. In C. Ragin (ed.) *Issues and Alternatives in Comparative Social Research* (Leiden: Brill), pp 154–171.

Chamberlayne, P. and King, A. (1996) Biographical approaches in comparative work: the 'Cultures of Care' project. In L. Hantrais and S. Mangen (eds) *Cross-National Research Methods in the Social Sciences* (London: Pinter), pp 95–104.

Dogan, M. and Pelassey, D. (1990) *How to Compare Nations* (Second Edition) (Chatham, USA: Chatham House).

Ferrari, V. (1990) Socio-legal concepts and their comparison. In E. Øyen (ed.) *Comparative Methodology. Theory and Practice in International Social Research* (London: Sage), pp 63–80.

Fielding, N.G. and Lee, R.M. (1998) *Computer Analysis and Qualitative Research* (London: Sage).

Griffin, L.J., Botsko, C., Wahl, A-M. and Isaac, L.W. (1991) Theoretical generality, case particularity: qualitative comparative analysis of trade union growth and decline. In C. Ragin (ed.) *Issues and Alternatives in Comparative Social Research* (Leiden: Brill), pp 110–135.

Jobert. A. (1996) Comparing education, training and employment in Germany, the United Kingdom and Italy. In L. Hantrais and S. Mangen (eds) *Cross-National Research Methods in the Social Sciences* (London: Pinter), pp 76–83.

Keman, H. (1993) Comparative politics: a distinctive approach to political science. In H. Keman (ed.) *Comparative Politics. New Directions in Theory and Method* (Amsterdam: VU University Press), pp 31–58.

Kohn, M.L. (1989) Cross-national research as an analytic strategy. In M.L. Kohn (ed.) *Cross-national Research in Sociology* (London: Sage), pp 77–103.

Nowak, S. (1989) Comparative studies and social theory. In M.L. Kohn (ed.) *Cross-national Research in Sociology* (London: Sage), pp 34–56.

Pitrou, A. (1994) Some initial thoughts on cross-national comparisons of family policy 'measures': beyond words and declarations of intent. *Cross-National Research Papers* **4**(3), 10–14.

Ragin, C. (1987) *The Comparative Method* (Los Angeles, CA: University of California Press).

Ragin, C. (1989) New directions in comparative research. In M.L. Kohn (ed.) *Cross-national Research in Sociology* (London: Sage), pp 57–76.

Rainbird, H. (1996) Negotiating a research agenda for comparisons of vocational training. In L. Hantrais and S. Mangen (eds) *Cross-National Research Methods in the Social Sciences* (London: Pinter), pp 109–119.

Richards, T.J. and Richards, L. (1991) The transformation of qualitative method: computational paradigms and research processes. In N. Fielding and R.M. Lee (eds) *Using Computers in Qualitative Research* (London: Sage), pp 38–53.

Rose, R. (1991) Comparing forms of comparative analysis. *Political Studies*, **39**(3), 446–462.

Rueschemeyer. D. (1991) Different methods – contradictory results? Research on development and democracy. In C. Ragin (ed.), *Issues and Alternatives in Comparative Social Research* (Leiden: Brill), pp 9–38.

Sartori, G. (1973) Faulty concepts. In P.G. Lewis and D.C. Potter (eds) *The Practice of Comparative Politics* (London: Longman/Open University Press), pp 181–218.

Seidel, J. (1991) Method and madness in the application of computer technology to qualitative data analysis. In N. Fielding and R.M. Lee (eds) *Using Computers in Qualitative Research* (London: Sage), pp 107–115.

Skocpol, T. (1984) Emerging agendas and recurrent strategies in historical sociology. In T. Skocpol (ed.) *Vision and Method in Historical Sociology* (Cambridge: Cambridge University Press), pp 356–391.

Soydan, H. (1996) Using the vignette method in cross-cultural comparison. In L. Hantrais and S. Mangen (eds) *Cross-National Research Methods in the Social Sciences* (London: Pinter), pp 120–128.

Teune, H. (1990) Comparing countries: lessons learned. In E. Øyen (ed.) *Comparative Methodology. Theory and Practice in International Social Research* (London: Sage), pp 38–62.

Wickham-Crowley, T. (1991) A qualitative comparative approach to Latin American revolutions. In C. Ragin (ed.) *Issues and Alternatives in Comparative Social Research* (Leiden: Brill), pp 82–109.

Combining quantitative and qualitative research methods in the study of international migration

ANN SINGLETON

Introduction

A major supplier of data on international migration in Europe is the Statistical Office of the European Communities (Eurostat). The Eurostat database is used by policy makers, researchers and journalists on a wide range of migration related topics, within individual member states and across the European Union (EU). Many of the problems with using this type of cross-national dataset on international migration have been documented in the literature (Salt *et al.* 1994, Singleton 1999). They are briefly outlined here, with reference to data on measurement of the flows of migrants, asylum seekers and labour migrants.

The database consists of a collection of national data supplied on an annual (and, in some cases, monthly) basis by the member states. Five broad categories of 'migration' data are produced: resident population by citizenship, international immigration and emigration, asylum, labour migration and acquisition of citizenship. The data, supplied by national statistical institutes and ministries, are products of more than 60 different legislative, administrative and data collection systems across the EU. Even the most efficient of these systems, which constitute the individual sources

Ann Singleton is on assignment to Eurostat, in Luxembourg, from the Centre for the Study of Social Exclusion and Social Injustice, School for Policy Studies, University of Bristol, 8 Priory Road, Bristol BS8 1TZ, UK; e-mail: a.singleton@wsel.lu. She is working with the Eurostat Population Team as an expert statistician on asylum and migration statistics. Her publications include (with J. Salt and J. Hogarth) *Europe's International Migrants. Data Sources, Patterns and Trends* (London: HMSO 1994), and Measuring international migration: the tools aren't up to the job, in D. Dorling and S. Simpson (eds), *Statistics in Society* (Arnold 1999), pp. 148–158.

at national level, record only fragments of the totality of human mobility across international borders. When the data they supply are aggregated in the international database, a complete picture of international migration in Europe does not emerge. The result is, rather, a series of overlapping snapshots taken at different times, with large gaps where data are not available on characteristics of migrants, or on whole groups of migrants, who do not fit into the definitions used in the recording systems. As all the original sources of migration data are national, no alternative international reference dataset exists which can provide a reference for checking the data. Despite considerable efforts within, and on behalf of, Eurostat to harmonize the aggregate datasets, most of the problems and inconsistencies that are generated at national level remain, and many migrants go unrecorded in any system or database.

Measuring the flows of migrants

A core problem in the data lies in the key concept of an 'international migrant'. The definition used by the United Nations of a migrant who lives in a country for one year or more, having previously lived outside that country for more than one year, is an unmeasurable variable in many reporting countries. National definitions in the recorded data range from residence periods of three months (Denmark), to six months (Netherlands), to the intention to stay more than one year (UK). Some definitional inconsistencies have been 'ironed out' in the aggregate tables by recalculations and the inclusion of Eurostat's estimated data, but most extractions of cross-national tabulations remain unharmonized. This means that even the most general statistical tables used to analyse patterns and trends of migration in Europe present an unclear picture of the reality of human mobility across borders.

For many researchers wishing to engage in cross-national social research, the broad overviews provided by aggregated tables do not offer adequate detail on the characteristics of migrants. Variables such as the age, sex and occupational status of migrants are requested on a regular basis. The cross-tabulations prove disappointing when discovered to be full of gaps where data are not available, either for a whole country, for a key variable, or for the most recent years. Unrealistic expectations on the part of individual researchers are compounded by the fact that research projects (including those commissioned by the institutions of the EU) do not necessarily take account of the lacunae in the datasets.

Similar problems are familiar to users of other types of statistics at European level. The free movement of goods across national borders has presented statisticians with the challenge of how to use national data to monitor dynamic international phenomena. Although these movements take place within a cross-national policy and legislative framework, for both types of movements, national systems are the sources of regulation and monitoring. One national system will rarely record the same level of imports as the level of exports reported by the corresponding country.

One example of the inconsistencies between reporting countries' data on immigration and emigration has been highlighted in a 'mirror study'[1] of data for Belgium and Italy. In matching the corresponding national data, Bisogno and Poulain (1999) have demonstrated that equivalent volumes of flows are rarely recorded, even by two countries that both use population registers as sources of international migration statistics. The numbers of Belgian and Italian citizens recorded as migrants between the two countries are substantially different for the same reporting periods.

The study of labour migration presents these data problems as well as others that are specific to the data type. All national datasets on labour migrants in the EU under-record or exclude EU nationals, due to the removal of administrative sources such as work permits (with the lifting of restrictions on their freedom to live and work throughout the EU). The temporary nature of many movements of labour migrants means that they may not appear at all in the residence records or employment registers of each member state. Combined with the existence of unrecorded labour migrants from outside the EU, it is difficult to acquire an accurate picture of the numbers of all non-nationals working within the EU and its constituent national states.

Data on asylum seekers

One type of national data in international databases commonly assumed to be harmonized in terms of definitions, is statistical information on asylum seeking derived from the records of national asylum procedures. This assumption is incorrect as asylum statistics, like other types of migration data from administrative sources, are the products of different types of national systems.

In each country it is usually the Ministry of the Interior which is responsible for the asylum process. Common definitions are presumed to exist in policy debates between the ministries and national governments but the data in cross-national datasets do not uniformly measure the same stages in asylum processes. This has consequences for research on any aspect of asylum seeking in Europe, and it adds to the problem that few countries are able to provide data for longitudinal studies of asylum seekers (van Dam and Erf 1998: 29).

When combined in a cross-national dataset, asylum application and decision data do present an apparently harmonized picture of asylum seeking across the EU. The data are, unfortunately, not entirely comparable. For example, data on asylum applicants should normally be on new (first) applications, but it is not always possible to distinguish these applications from second or subsequent applications. The application data may refer to individual applicants, or to cases that include dependants (as is the case for the UK). The definition of a dependant varies between member states: sometimes minor dependants are included and sometimes not. Decision data reflect the complexities of the decision-making processes involved in the determination or rejection of refugee status. Cases may be heard at first, second and subsequent instances in the legal process and it is not always evident which stage of the process is recorded in the data.

Statistics on the recognition of refugee status under the international definition set out in the Geneva Convention are not always tabulated in the same way by different countries. The different legislative frameworks create a confusing picture even in the most apparently straightforward tables. Recognition of *de facto* status, the use of temporary protection regimes and different reporting practices result in different categories being used to record people at similar stages in these processes across the EU.

Although data collection systems have responded to the needs imposed by the Dublin Convention (on the transfer of asylum seekers within the EU back to the EU country they first entered), these data may be the only type of asylum data that can be considered harmonized. This is of little use to researchers, as the data are not publicly available.

The examples of problems with the different types of data outlined above give some indication of the task facing a researcher who wishes to engage in quantitative analysis of patterns and trends in migration. These problems of incomparability and availability also impact on the possibilities for migration related research which is conducted using other types of research methods. It is often the case, though, that small-scale in-depth studies which employ different types of qualitative methodologies start with the identification of 'target groups', using statistical data. In the absence of an understanding of the limitations of international migration data, the consequences for migration related research are that, too often, research studies are conceived, funding contracts are won and projects almost completed, before the statistical bases underpinning key assumptions have been tested.

Overcoming the constraints

It is possible to overcome some of the limitations outlined here. This requires careful and appropriate selection of the data, the choices being informed by recently available documentation and metadata. Having outlined the main causes of the unharmonized nature of data on international migration, it is important to recognize that they do provide a framework within which trends can be identified, using cross-national historical time series. Data on the resident population by citizenship, for example, show over time the changes in composition of different groups of foreign nationals within each country. Asylum data provide information on the citizenship of applicants, reflecting the effects of political events and the effectiveness of policies to regulate and control the numbers of applicants. Data on acquisition of citizenship are used (appropriately or not) as indicators of the degree of success of integration policies.

Carefully selected sources and available data, however, do permit the identification of indicators of change that may be used to inform research aims. Eurostat's cross-national dataset, for example, includes more complete data for some countries than for others on workers from non-EU countries. National sources range from those such as the Office de migrations internationales (OMI) records in France, derived from the records of medical examinations of non-EU workers entering the country, to the microcensus in Germany. The microcensus data include a sample of the whole resident population and provide information on the citizenship, sex and age of resident migrants. Cross-tabulations of these variables with occupational status and geographical region do not exist at EU level, but selection of such data types from different national sources can provide data with which to inform cross-national studies across a few of the member states. In addition, the Labour Force Survey, which is conducted in all member states, is a source that provides a reasonably good estimate of the total numbers of non-EU workers in the EU, although it becomes less accurate or useful at any level of disaggregation by citizenship (Salt and Singleton 1994). Census data and population register data on the resident population by citizenship, sex and age reveal changes through time in the numbers of women from non-EU countries living in different EU countries. If the information from these different sources is combined with an analysis of the changing economic relationship between EU and non-EU countries, emerging patterns in the labour market may be identified which are not yet evident in the labour data for that country.

An essential element in approaching the selection of migration data is to be aware of the precise detail in their differences and incompatibility. Eurostat has produced a series of working papers in which the different datasets on migration have been documented. The documentation relevant to each data extraction provides a guide to the content of the statistical tables. The working papers are based on a set of documentation and metadata which describe, on a country by country basis, the nature of the sources used for each type of data. The definitions used by each ministry and national statistical institute are listed, and the particular peculiarities of data that occur from year to year, for a whole range of reasons, are described. This documentation, which is freely available from Eurostat, should be consulted in the preliminary stages of planning a research proposal. It allows the user to select data with as complete a picture as possible of which groups of migrants are included and which are not. The example provided above, of combining different sources of labour migration data, would for instance be facilitated by the use of the documentation of the labour data in Eurostat's database (Clarke *et al.* 1998).

There are indications that some types of international migration data in Europe may become harmonized in the future. The co-ordination of international practice and policy areas is also likely to stimulate the production of new categories of migration data. New policy areas related to the control of immigration are, for example, resulting in proposals to harmonize data collection systems within the applicant countries of Central Europe, where new administrative systems are being introduced along with computerized systems of data collection and the use of harmonized definitions. It can be confidently predicted, however that any movement towards harmonization will, according to the sources used in each national system, continue to be counter-balanced by an uneven coverage of groups and characteristics for each of the categories of migrants recorded. The big gap will continue to be, by definition, the absence of data on undocumented and/or illegal migration. There is little point in attempting a quantitative approach to cross-national research on these groups of migrants.

Possibilities do arise, however, in qualitative studies of the informal economies of local areas to exploit this type of data.

Conclusions

The subject matter of international migration is cross-national in scope, whilst international migration statistics are the products of national government ministries, administrations and statistical institutes. The counting tools used to measure the phenomena associated with the movement of people across borders are limited, conceptually, linguistically and within the legal definitions applied by each national jurisdiction. This creates a constraint in the area of cross-national policy development as well as a challenge to researchers attempting to measure and analyse patterns of migration across Europe and between EU member states and other countries.

In the field of migration policy, harmonization has taken place in legal and policy terms only in the general approach to controlling the immigration of third-country nationals to the EU. General migration policy development has been limited within the broad common aims of governments to control immigration and to tackle the root causes of emigration pressure from the 'sending' countries. These policy developments have had little impact on the structures and systems of statistical data production within member states. Exceptions to this pattern lie in the response of the applicant countries of Central Europe to EU demands for the use of harmonized concepts and definitions in the fields of Justice and Home Affairs.

Migration involves many complicated and inter-related social processes, and migratory movements are motivated by multiple reasons, usually a combination of economic and social concerns. Temporary migrations, or those repeated more frequently than on a seasonal basis, may, paradoxically, be the only constant in the fragmented lives of migrant labourers who often live in more than one place of residence (in different countries) which they regard as their home. Few opportunities arise to record these elements of migration in the existing data collections and those of the foreseeable future.

For researchers in the field of social policy, harmonization of immigration control will not necessarily result in richer sources of statistical data. Development is needed of new migrant typologies, independent of, and not bounded by the definitions used in existing data categories, in national and international databases; nor by the policy concerns of ministries of the interior. The categories used in official statistics–labour migrants, asylum seekers, immigrants and emigrants–often conceal as much as they reveal about migration. Many of the new migration flows in Europe are not captured in the typologies which largely appear to reflect the policy concerns of national states since the 1950s. In the changing economic, social and legal systems within Europe during the 1990s, it is apparent that new typologies are needed which include the variety of human mobility across-national borders. An early prototype of such a typology was carried out for Eurostat (Singleton and Salt 1999). Subsequent attempts to develop the work have foundered at the point of resource allocation, the positivist imperative still driving a thirst for statistical data in migration related research.

Data availability and policy concerns that underpin data production have historically restricted the research agenda. However, increasing numbers of research projects concerned with cross-national policy issues are focusing on new and emerging patterns of migration. If the data are used as indicators of emerging trends, rather than as accurate quantitative measurements of the actual size of flows, they present the potential to spot new characteristics of the recorded migrant population. The use of documentation and metadata is essential in this process. Combined with analysis of the political, economic and social processes of globalization, this may provide a route for identifying new migrant groups, and help to free migration research from the conceptual limitations imposed by existing statistical data. The questions asked of the data are more important than the answers they provide.

Acknowledgements

Research teams at University College London (Migration Research Unit) and the Netherlands Indisciplinary Demographic Institute produced most of the documentation of Eurostat's database on international migration. The views expressed here are the author's own.

Notes

1. A 'mirror study' consists simply of analysing corresponding data presented in a 'double matrix' table in which each cell contains the corresponding data for 'arrivals' and 'dispatches'. The data are also presented in graphs. Alajääskö (1997: 4) in a study which compared intra-European trade statistics on 'arrivals' and 'dispatches' showed that both the level and the trend of discrepancies seemed to remain stable over time.

References

Alajääskö, P. (1997) *Eurostat Mirror Leaflet* (Luxembourg: Eurostat).
Bisogno, E. and Poulain, M. (1999) La fiabilité de la mesure des courants de migration internationale entre la Belgique et l'Italie. *Eurostat Working Papers: Population and Social Conditions*, 3/1999/ E. No. 4 (Luxembourg: Eurostat).
Clarke, J., Clarke, M., van Dam E., Salt, I., Salt, J., Cantisani, G., Eding, H. and Singleton, A. (1998) Documentation of Eurostat's database on international migration: labour data. *Eurostat Working papers: Population and Social Conditions*, 3/1998/E/no. 16 (Luxembourg: Eurostat).
Salt, J. and Singleton, A. (1993) Comparison and evaluation of the Labour Force Survey and Regulation 311/76 as sources on the foreign employed population in the EC. *Report to the Eurostat Working Party on Migration Statistics* (Luxembourg).
Salt, J., Singleton, A. and Hogarth, J. (1994) *Europe's International Migrants. Data Sources, Patterns and Trends* (London: HMSO).
Singleton, A. (1999) Measuring international migration: the tools aren't up to the job. In D. Dorling, and S. Simpson (eds) *Statistics in Society* (London: Arnold), pp 148–158.
Singleton, A. and Salt, J. (1999) Analysis and forecasting of international migration by major groups. *Report to Eurostat* (Luxembourg), forthcoming.
van Dam, E. and Erf, R. (1998) Asylum-seekers and refugees, a statistical report. Vol. 3: Central European Countries. *Eurostat Working Papers: Population and social conditions*, 3/1998/E. No.19 (Luxembourg: Eurostat).

Cross-national qualitative research: accommodating ideals and reality

MONIKA ZULAUF

Introduction

This article considers problems of gaining access to data in cross-national research and their impact on the research design and process of a study about the occupational integration of European Union (EU) migrants in Britain, Germany and Spain. Little consensus exists among academics as to whether cross-national research has features different from research in general (Øyen 1990). It is more widely accepted, however, that cross-national projects may require compromises beyond those of single-country studies (Hantrais and Mangen 1996). Scrutiny of the extensive literature on research methods shows that very few studies have analysed the cross-national research process with reference to migrants. Not only is the literature scarce, but its focus has been on approaches, the theoretical and epistemological problems in conducting cross-national comparative research, and on projects undertaken by research teams based in one or more countries. This article contributes to the growing body of literature on small-scale cross-national research practice by a lone researcher. It provides an account of the methodological aims and reveals the compromises that were needed in the research design as a result of access problems.

Monika Zulauf is a research fellow in the Faculty of Humanities and Social Science, South Bank University, 103 Borough Road, London SE1 0AA, UK; e-mail: zulaufm@sbu.ac.uk. Her research interests are in European policy studies, with particular reference to migration and employment. Her recent publications include Time organization and the integration of EU migrant professionals. *Time and Society*, 1997, 6(2/3), 151–170, and Free movement in the European Union: experiences of nurses. *European Nurse*, 1998, 3(3), 143–157.

Methodological aims

The objectives of the research were threefold: to identify the organizational, practical, cultural and attitudinal barriers faced by EU migrants when seeking and taking up work in other member states; to investigate the extent to which these restrictions influenced migrants' employment experiences in access to jobs commensurate with their qualifications and skills obtained prior to migration; to examine their integration in the work environment and access to career progression within host countries; and, finally, to establish the implications for cross-national mobility of qualified workers in the EU. Initially, secondary sources were reviewed, including reports and official documents by national and international institutions and statistical sources, drawing on a variety of theoretical perspectives, concepts and studies on national, intra-EU and international labour migration and on migrant women's situation in labour markets. This review contributed to the formulation of research questions to be investigated and the analytical framework.

Migrant women in the nursing and banking professions in Britain, Germany and Spain, who were single and childless at the time of migration, were chosen for an investigation of the research questions posed. These groups and countries were selected for a number of reasons. Literature on the Single European Market (SEM) (Cecchini 1989, Commission of the European Communities 1988, 1989) pointed to a concentration of employment growth in the private services sector, particularly financial services. Greater labour demand was also anticipated in health, education and social services (Kottis 1991). Women were assumed to benefit particularly from developments in the latter services. The majority of employees in the health and financial sectors are female. By including the public services sector and by choosing to investigate women, this study filled an important gap in existing research. Single childless migrant women were chosen because they were expected to be the most mobile among women and, therefore, most likely to take up opportunities in another country. In addition, single migrant women cannot usually rely on a partner's income. The likelihood of entering employment in another member state, and seeking to maintain their professional status was, therefore, expected to be higher than for migrant women accompanying their partners. Moreover, knowledge about the position of single migrant women in EU labour markets is an under-researched area (Millar 1990).

Comparisons of occupations and occupational levels are very difficult cross-nationally and require close matching of the phenomena under investigation (Crompton and Le Feuvre 1992). By choosing the banking profession in the financial sector and the nursing profession in the health sector, the occupational categories were narrowed down to one career structure in each sector and, therefore, to a considerably smaller range of qualifications. A narrow focus was considered to be particularly important in the measurement of the effects of migration on migrants' employment status and in the comparison of employment progression between countries.

Germany, Britain and Spain were selected because they joined the EU at different periods of the integration process since the Treaty of Rome: 1957, 1973 and 1986 respectively. Moreover, these countries display different attitudes towards European integration (see Zulauf 1996). Most importantly, in a number of respects, the three countries differ in training and employment systems, the organization of work, and supply and demand factors between the two professions. Such variations were expected to influence the migrants' experiences in member states. It was anticipated that the findings would highlight the remaining obstacles, and ultimately policy requirements, for achieving genuine freedom of movement within the EU. Ackers (in this volume) makes a similar point when she refers to the two dimensions of context in migration studies, namely variables applying to the countries of emigration and destination.

Existing information on EU migrants working in other member states is limited. About two million EU migrants are employed within the EU, but neither EU nor national employment statistics specify the proportion of EU migrants in particular employment subsectors. The collection and availability of statistical data varies significantly between countries. Complete official statistics are not available and, the data available lacks reliability (see Singleton in this volume). The historical, cultural and administrative structures specific to each country, and different conceptual histories and current policy frameworks make the availability and comparability of statistical data problematic for users and limit cross-national comparisons (Desrosières 1996, Evans 1996). For example, nursing migrants have to register their qualifications to be able to work in EU countries, and relevant statistics should, therefore, be available from the registration bodies. The British authority was able to provide figures on the number of migrants who had their qualifications verified (UKCC 1992). However, the statistics do not show whether migrants actually entered the country and took up employment. In Germany and Spain, nursing registration is decentralized to regional and local levels, which made the task of obtaining statistics impossible. Letters sent to 38 registration authorities in Germany indicated that only 12 could provide information. There was also evidence of the unsuccessful attempts by the European Commission to establish the numbers of EU migrants in the various health sector professions in EU countries (letter from the German Ministry of Health, 27 April 1993). Only five countries had provided the data. Britain, though not Germany and Spain, was among these countries. In the wake of these findings, it was decided not to contact the large number of registration bodies in Spain, since information was expected to be incomplete.

The absence of statistical data on EU migrants working in various employment subsectors in EU countries limits the possibility of undertaking extensive quantitative studies in this field. Evidence has to be collected on the basis of small-scale qualitative and highly selective studies. However, in the present case, other more specific reasons explain the choice of a qualitative approach. Firstly, existing research on EU labour migrants was limited and focused on the unskilled and semi-skilled mainly in the manufacturing industry. Skilled/qualified migrants and the services sector had hardly received any attention. The research, therefore, needed to address contextual questions such as the nature of the migrants' experiences. Secondly, the study aimed in part at identifying barriers that derived from attitudes, perceptions and behaviour. This required attention to diagnostic questions. Thirdly, the study aimed at examining existing policies and practices, and contributing to the development of actions still required to achieve genuine freedom of movement. The research, therefore, had to include evaluative questions such as the effect of policies and practices on migrants' experiences and behaviour, if policy recommendations were to be developed.

Sampling method

In addressing the research questions, the understanding of processes was more important than obtaining a representative sample of the EU migrant population. This can be best achieved by in-depth interviews of a small sample (Arber 1993). Sixty interviews (ten in each profession and country) with the main target group was decided upon. Moreover, it was thought to be necessary to interview not only migrants but also representatives of regulatory institutions, and some managers and colleagues to establish subjective and objective barriers to the integration of EU migrants.

A clustered design was used to compile the main sample. This approach uses more than one stage of selection and is intended to reduce time and cost (Arber 1993) and particular consideration was given to sampling equivalence (for a discussion see Harkness in this volume). The first stage was to decide on the sampling area in each country. The financial sector was used to determine the selection because hospitals are less restricted in their choice of location. It was decided to restrict the study to the financial centres in each country, namely London, Frankfurt and Madrid. Although this option was expected to make the findings less interesting in terms of factors such as different attitudes towards foreigners than if they had been used in the selection criteria, it had other benefits. For example, it reduced the number of exogenous variables, and the cost and time in undertaking the fieldwork. However, the sampling method was later changed for the reasons explained below.

Organizational, practical, cultural and attitudinal barriers can best be investigated at the workplace level. The second stage in the selection was, therefore, to choose the type of institution. Arber (1993) argues that stratification within each stage of selection maximizes precision. The aim was to obtain the sample in a small number of organizations in each country. For the financial sector, private commercial banks were chosen. The types of banks included within this group are fairly similar between the three countries. They are part of the private banking system, and they usually fall under the same collective agreement within countries. For Germany, commercial banks include the large universal banks, regional banks and other private banks; for Britain, high street banks and subsidiaries, and wholesale banks (accepting houses and consortium banks); and for Spain national, regional and local commercial banks.

Foreign commercial banks were not included because, in terms of employment, the law of their own country tends to apply.

For the health sector, public sector hospitals were chosen because hospital ownership varies significantly between the three countries. Britain, for example, has abandoned charitable hospitals, but they still play a significant role in Spain and Germany. Public hospitals included National Health Service hospitals in Britain, regional and local authority hospitals in Germany, and social security, provincial and municipal hospitals in Spain. It was planned to draw the sample from three types of public hospitals: general hospitals, teaching hospitals and specialist hospitals of more than 500 beds. This choice was to ensure the acquisition of general and specialized nurses among the target group. Larger hospitals were chosen because of the higher likelihood of finding EU migrants in these settings, and obtaining the sample from a small number of hospitals.[1]

Gaining access

Access to interviewees can be a time-consuming task in research. Whether the researcher acts independently or as a representative of an institution, and whether the targeted organization is a public or private body can be crucial in obtaining access to gatekeepers and respondents (Peace 1997). The process of gaining access to interviewees can create additional difficulty and inconvenience in cross-national research.

Initially, letters were sent to ten organizations in each employment sector and country. Personnel managers were informed in broad outline of the nature of the study, the type and number of interviewees required, the funding body, and were given the assurance of confidentiality. Three weeks after the date of the letter, only a small number of replies had been received. One hospital in Germany, and one bank in both Germany and Britain agreed to participate. Reminder letters and additional letters to further organizations in each employment sector and country were distributed. Some weeks later, the response was still minimal. The participation of one hospital in Britain and three more in Germany was obtained. For Germany, this outcome meant that more than the required number of nursing migrants had been found. All were accepted to cater for any unforeseen problems during the interviewing stage. By then, only two responses had been received from Spain. Neither employed any EU migrants. The sampling area in Spain was therefore extended to the coastal cities of Barcelona, Valencia and Alicante, which also have a high proportion of EU residents.

At the same time, letters were followed up by phone calls in all three countries. The response was generally negative. Some hospitals in Britain did not hold information on EU nurses centrally. Others said that too much work was involved finding the migrants. Others, perhaps understandably, declined a request for lists of hospital wards so that they could be contacted directly. In the meantime, a relatively large number of Spanish hospitals and banks had begun to respond to letters. None of them employed any EU migrants, though some hospitals were willing to discuss the topic.

Some banks in Britain and Germany were unwilling to participate, either because of the time involved or because they could not see any benefit to themselves. A number of bank managers were willing to discuss the theme, but not participate, apparently because their computer database on employees could not provide information as to whether migrants had received their training abroad or in the country. Informal knowledge about the target group among staff was returned with excuses that suggested wariness to participate in the study. Others declined on the basis that they only employed one or two female EU migrants. When it was suggested that this number would be sufficient, no reply was received. The banking section of the German federal employment bureau confirmed that banking was a relatively closed sector. It was pointed out that most appointments occurred internally and were arranged by management, and few openings were likely to exist for EU migrants in Germany. A similar point was put forward by the British Banking, Insurance and Finance Union (BIFU). As Hornsby-Smith (1993: 54) points out 'for some closed groups research may, ideologically, be anathema. Others see research as a threat because of the repercussions it might have inside the research setting, it disrupts operational routines, there are fears of exploitation or it may result in damaging disclosures'.

Compromises in the research methods

Access problems led to the decision to abandon the study of the organizational context. This change in the research design, ultimately, affected the outcome. Thus, the main hypothesis, defined from the analysis of the literature, had to be modified. Originally, the aim had been to examine to what extent female EU migrants experienced the dual disadvantage of gender and foreigner status in their occupational integration in host countries, and to establish differences between the occupational groups, nationalities and countries. These issues were to be explored in a number of workplaces in the three countries under study. However, an investigation within an organizational context would have required multiple data about the organizations, such as employment and career policies, statistics, management policies and practices towards (migrant) women workers at workplace level, and a survey interviewing multiple informants at each participating institution (Hakim 1997). The abandonment of the research in an organizational context meant, instead, that national labour markets had to provide the main contextual frame of reference for the analysis of the research questions. Explaining and interpreting diverse local findings on two professions in a national and cross-national context required the consideration of a wide variety of variables and proved complicated. The complexities, but also advantages, of a societal approach over others in cross-national research are documented by Hantrais and Mangen (both in this issue) and do not need further elaboration here.

The time and expense involved in sending out further letters and phoning organizations abroad led to the decision to travel to the countries and complete the sample through the snowball method. This method involves the personal recommendation of a contact. Sample members are found by asking people whether they know anyone with the required characteristics (Arber 1993). Members of the target groups were obtained through phoning banks and hospitals in the chosen cities, visiting cultural centres and language schools who offered to advertise the study on notice boards and in classes, and from recommendations of research participants already acquired. A potential weakness of the snowball method is, of course, that it only includes individuals within a specific network of people. Research findings and subsequent analysis may, therefore, be subject to bias (Arber 1993). However, due to the problems already mentioned, it was the only feasible method for compiling the sample.

To compensate for the change in the research method, the sample was obtained at several levels of the employment process and, as far as possible, within the same organization. Thus, a number of employers had agreed to discuss the topic without offering access to migrants. Such offers were taken up and, through informal inquiries, migrants were found and interviewed from within the organizations. In some other cases, native workers in the employment sector were recommended by friends and from other persons and institutions contacted. With the completion of the interviews, it was proposed to make contacts with employers and/or migrants. However, on some occasions, the interviews with migrants and/ or native workers took place without the knowledge of management. The adoption of such a 'flexible approach' meant that, not infrequently, employers, migrants and native workers were interviewed from within the organization, but employers could not be asked for statistical data to avoid raising suspicion. Through the use of the snowball method, and overt and covert methods of investigation, a sufficient number of migrants and other groups were obtained for the research. However, the change in the method also meant that the migrant group, the sampling area and institutions had to be extended in each country.

A small number of nationalities from countries other than those under investigation were incorporated. Cross-national comparison is particularly difficult if the group studied comes from a variety of countries. It was virtually an impossible research task to try and obtain information on the background, systems of training and employment, and work organization of all the different countries from which the migrants came. The majority of them had, in fact, moved between the three countries selected, and explanations could be contextualized for migrant women from Britain, Germany and Spain. Migrants from other countries remained on the margins of the analysis, though their experiences were used to substantiate some of the arguments. Any findings and conclusions drawn, however, might have become subject to bias. The change in the sampling method and expansion of geographical areas obviously added to the cost and time in conducting the research. It also added to the complexity of the analysis because of the differences between local labour market features and situations within countries. For instance, registration procedures for nurses are decentralized in Germany and Spain. On the basis of this factor alone, the experiences of migrants could vary significantly within these two countries.

A researcher's institution and its reputation may help to facilitate access, or at least get the researcher to the stage of negotiation (Peace 1997). In cross-national research, such factors may be irrelevant if the institution is unknown abroad. The problem was compounded by the fact that, in all the countries in the study, the researcher was 'foreign' to the personnel managers approached. Although few in Germany would have assumed the researcher to be of foreign nationality, they were contacted via a foreign institution and country. In Britain, the institution was generally recognized, but the researcher could not deny her foreignness on the basis of her name and accent, often requiring lengthy explanations with regards to herself rather than that of the research. In Spain, the researcher was foreign on all accounts.

The more 'relaxed' attitude by Spanish institutions may have played a role in the poor response to earlier written inquiries. However, once in the country, access was no longer a problem. In fact, the fieldwork in Spain was completed in the shortest period of the three countries even though, prior to arrival, no interviews had been arranged nor migrants found. Whilst this success may be attributed, partly, to a different cultural approach towards communication methods and expectations in terms of responding to written requests (Levine 1987), the fixed period in the country may have been a contributing factor. Once the period of stay in the country was known to people, respondents made themselves available at very short notice in both Spain and Germany, often the very next day, and, unlike in Britain, postponing or cancelling appointments was not an issue. Perhaps the knowledge that the researcher lived in the country may have extended the fieldwork period in Britain beyond the initial time planned. In Spain, the researcher's nationality turned out to be a distinct advantage, particularly with banking employers. Employers spoke highly of the German training and employment systems and its economic performance. They did not just simply respond to questions related to the study, but initiated informal discussions about other issues, both work and non-work related, which eased the communication process immensely. When aware of this advantage, the researcher made certain that her country of origin was notified to the other party in telephone negotiations. Moreover, Spanish people, at whatever employment level, were highly tolerant and open-minded towards speakers of other European languages. The much written about language barriers in cross-national research, particularly when engaging in interviewing (Hantrais and Ager 1985, Hantrais and Mangen 1996, Mangen in this volume), was not an issue in this research, even though the researcher was not fluent in Spanish. This tolerance was also highlighted frequently by migrant interviewees.

Achieving the sample

In total, the research drew upon several sources of data: 119 interviews and group discussions, observational notes, printed sources and statistics by local institutions, official documents, statistics and secondary data. The empirical aim was to collect data on objective and subjective barriers to the occupational integration of EU migrants in European labour markets. The objective barriers were identified by talking to as many different people as possible involved in the employment process. It was feared that the quality of information collected by a foreign interviewer might suffer, particularly when using highly unstructured interviews (Mangen in this volume). In view of this concern and the variety of groups and nationalities participating in the study, semi-structured questionnaires and structured interview guides were chosen. All the questions and coded responses were put onto cards and given to the interviewees. This choice had been made for a number of reasons, most importantly, it was a help to the migrants who did not have an advanced knowledge of the language of the host country. All questionnaires and cards were prepared in three languages. Though this was extremely time-consuming in the preparation stage, it helped smooth the interviewing process, as the researcher did not get into the situation of needing to search for the exact translation during the interview. Achieving linguistic, functional and conceptual equivalence is one of the most difficult tasks in cross-national research (Mangen in this volume). The questionnaires and interview guides in Spanish were, therefore, prepared with the help of a native speaker to ensure that the best possible equivalence was being used. Most interviews were taped to assist the subsequent coding and analytical processes. In addition, observational notes were kept during the period of preparation and conduct of the fieldwork as another means of obtaining objective information. The methods used to collect the data for the study can be summarized as follows:

- **Secondary data**–published national and international sources, including reports and official documents and statistics.
- **Primary data**–documents and statistics supplied by regulatory bodies and employers; observational notes.

<u>Interview data</u>:
regulatory institutions	17 individual interviews
employers	19 individual interviews
migrants	2 pilot interviews and
	60 individual interviews
native workers	21 individual interviews and
	group discussions.

Conclusion

This paper has outlined the problems of access in cross-national research, and the consequences for the research design and process. The paper demonstrates that the ideals set out in the planning stage of the project had to be compromised in the actual methodology finally used. The gap between the ideal and the reality was most likely exacerbated by the cross-national aspect of the study. As already argued by Hantrais (in this volume), 'the choices of units and levels of analysis, and variables in cross-national comparisons are generally constrained, if not imposed by external factors'.

It was found that employers had little interest in providing access to migrant employees. This may have been partly for economic reasons, though wariness was clearly identified in the negotiations for gaining access. Some of the problems may also be experienced in a single-country study. However, in a cross-national study, the researcher has far less opportunity to develop 'relationships' with gatekeepers and potential interviewees, as much of the negotiation over access is done in writing or by phone and not in meetings. The experience in Spain confirms what Peace (1997: 31) has claimed: 'in the end negotiations over access have to come down to face-to-face discussions'. Access to respondents in this study was difficult because of the absence of statistical data on EU migrants working in employment subsectors in EU member states, denial of access to organizations, workload, inconvenience, caution and distrust, lack of interest and last minute withdrawal from the study. As a result, the researcher was forced into what Hornsby-Smith (1993) calls overt and covert methods of investigation. Problems of access affected the research in two main ways: they influenced the research process, and the design and outcome of the study. These obstacles had an impact on the research process because negotiations over access were not simply a matter of a few weeks but required constant flexibility and adaptation throughout the planning and fieldwork period. The problems that arose added significantly to time and cost, much beyond the funds received for the study. And finally, the research questions had to be analysed with reference to national rather than subnational and national environments.

On reflection, two changes to the methodology could have eased the research process. Given the lack of statistical data on EU migrants working in various employment subsectors, any attempt to obtain the sample through systematic selection should have been rejected at the outset. Snowballing would seem to afford the best methodological choice for a study on EU migration. Moreover, greater flexibility towards changing part of the methodology, for example, the abandonment of interviews with one of the groups other than the main target group could have freed time to gain access to a more ideal sample.

Notes

1. For reasons of reliability and completeness national sampling frames were used to contact employers: the Bankers Almanac (UK), the Banken-Ortslexikon (D) and the Registros de Entidades de Crédito (E) for the banking sector; and the Hospital Yearbook (UK), Ärztebuch (D) and Hospitales de España (E) for the health sector. Systematic selection was used to obtain a simple random sample. The type of institutions in the selected areas were numbered and sample numbers were selected by a fixed sampling interval.

References

Arber, S. (1993) The research process. In N. Gilbert (ed.) *Researching Social Life* (London: Sage), pp 32–50.

Cecchini, P. (1989) *The European Challenge. 1992. The Benefits of a Single Market* (Aldershot: Wildwood House).

Commission of the European Communities (1988) *The Social Dimension of the Internal Market. Social Europe* (Luxembourg: Office for Official Publications of the European Communities).

Commission of the European Communities (1989) *Employment in Europe*. COM (89) 399 final (Luxembourg: Office for Official Publications of the European Communities).

Crompton, R. and Le Feuvre, N. (1992) Gender and bureaucracy: women in finance in Britain and France. In M. Savage and A.Witz (eds) *Gender and Bureaucracy* (Oxford: Blackwell), pp 94–120.

Desrosières, A. (1996) Statistical traditions: an obstacle to international comparisons?. In L. Hantrais and S. Mangen (eds) *Cross-National Research Methods in the Social Sciences* (London/New York: Pinter), pp 17–27.

Evans, M. (1996) Exploring statistics and national rules on social security. In L. Hantrais and S. Mangen (eds) *Cross-National Research Methods in the Social Sciences* (London/New York: Pinter), pp 138–147.

Hakim, C. (1997) *Research Design* (London: Routledge).

Hantrais, L. and Ager, D. (1985) The language barrier to effective cross-national research. *Doing Cross-National Research. Cross-National Research Papers* 1(1), 29–40.

Hantrais, L. and Mangen, S. (1996) Method and management of cross-national social research. In L. Hantrais and S. Mangen (eds) *Cross-National Research Methods in the Social Sciences* (London/New York: Pinter), pp 1–12.

Hornsby-Smith, M. (1993) Gaining access. In N. Gilbert (ed.) *Researching Social Life* (London: Sage), pp 52–67.

Kottis, A. (1991) Single European labour market equality between women and men. *International Journal of Manpower*, **12**(3), 3–8.

Levine, R. (1987) Coping with the silent language in cross-national research. *Doing Cross-National Research. Cross-National Research Papers*, **1**(3), 27–33.

Millar, J (1990) *The Socio-Economic Situation of Solo Women in Europe. Revised Final Report of the European Commission* (University of Bath: Centre for the Analysis of Social Policy).

Øyen, E. (1990) The imperfections of comparisons. In E. Øyen (ed.), *Comparative Methodology* (London: Sage), pp 1–18.

Peace, S. (1997) Negotiating. In P. Shakespeare, D. Atkinson and S. French (eds) *Reflecting on Research Practice* (Buckingham: Open University Press), pp 25–35.

UKCC (1992) Statistical analysis of the Council's professional register 1 April 1991 to 31 March 1992. *International Statistics*, Vol. 3, July (London: United Kingdom Central Council for Nursing, Midwifery and Health Visiting), pp 1–16.

Zulauf, M. (1996) *The Occupational Integration of Female European Union Migrants in Britain, Germany and Spain: A Case Study of the Nursing and Banking Professions*. Doctoral Thesis (London: London School of Economics).

Context, culture and values in migration research on children within the European Union

LOUISE ACKERS

Introduction

This paper describes the approach used in a comparative project concerned with evaluating the impact of migration on the citizenship status and experiences of children. The project examined the legal status of children in European Union (EU) migrant families, their participation in, and response to, migration decisions and the impact of migration on social status, kinship networks, language and identity. In addition to these objectives, the project sought to develop and evaluate an approach to comparative research involving children. Data was collected at a number of levels, including the evaluation of European Community law, secondary analysis of migration statistics and interviews with children and parents in Greece, Portugal, Sweden and the UK. The project was developed in close collaboration with partners in these four countries.

The paper focuses on two aspects of the project's operationalization that pose important and interesting challenges to comparative inquiry. Firstly, it discusses the relevance of current debates (around contextualiza-

Louise Ackers is Deputy Director of the Centre for the Study of Law in Europe, University of Leeds, Leeds LS2 9JT, UK. Her research interests are in European law and social policy, particularly in the field of internal migration. She is the co-ordinator of a project entitled, 'Children, Citizenship and Internal Migration in the EU' which is co-funded by the Nuffield Foundation and the European Commission. Her recent publications include H.L. Ackers, *Shifting Spaces. Women, Citizenship and Migration within the European Union* (Policy Press, 1998).

tion and culture-boundedness) for comparative research on migration. Many migrants move, over their life-course, not only once but on a number of occasions and often to different destinations. In addition, many of the children of migrants live in families of dual nationality with relatives and affective ties in a number of countries. Context, as a source of values and reference points, thus becomes a highly complex matter. The second challenge concerns the limited attention, within existing comparative research, to the situation of children. At national level, increasing interest in childhood as an area of research has precipitated a concern with issues of method and approach, but little attempt has been made to assess the viability and transferability of such methodological developments to cross-national research.

Context and culture in migration research

International migration research is, by definition, comparative. That said, the interdisciplinary nature of migration research and its domination by the disciplines of geography and economics have led to a variety of approaches (Ackers 1998, Boyle *et al.* 1998, Kelson and DeLaet 1999). The project described here is concerned with the relationship between migration and citizenship. As such, it borrows from both migration studies and comparative social policy analysis. The purpose in this section is to consider the relevance of recent debates, within the field of comparative social policy, around contextualization and culture-boundedness for research on intra-Community migration. In particular, it focuses on two dimensions of special relevance to migration research. The first concerns the problems of identifying the relevant policy context in situations where supranational and domestic policy are inextricably linked. The second considers the importance of extending the scope of culture-boundedness beyond the explanation of policy inputs to the citizen/user interface in order to advance our understanding of policy impact and citizenship experience.

Problems of contextualization in supranational policy evaluation

Traditionally, comparative social policy analysis has sought to compare aspects of social policy in two or more national contexts. In that sense, the nation state constitutes an important frame of reference. International migration research, however, demands consideration of the relationship between several layers of context. The researcher engaging in policy evaluation at comparative level needs to integrate an understanding of these different 'layers' of policy formulation, implementation and outcome. The focus of this project on Community law draws attention to the political, fiscal and normative variables guiding policy evolution and implementation at supranational level, including the fundamental objectives underpinning the free movement provisions and their interpretation by the European Court of Justice (Ackers 1998). It also demands an awareness of policy implementation by member states and the interface of free movement rights with domestic social policy. If a child moves to a country such as Sweden, which has effectively implemented the Directive on the education of children of migrant workers (Council Directive 77/486), it will, for example, benefit from the right to extra language support both in Swedish and its mother tongue, and also from the more progressive domestic policy on children's rights (Pringle 1998).

The principle of subsidiarity not only shapes the distribution of responsibilities and powers between the European Union (EU) and its member states, it also determines spatial access to social goods within domestic jurisdictions, resulting in problems of territorial injustice and uneven provision (Spicker 1991, Ackers and Abbott 1996). Access to material and social support for migrant children is thus, to a significant extent, influenced by regional location. In Athens, for example, services for children and migrant families are far better developed than in more remote areas of Greece. In the UK, service provision in policy areas in which local authorities retain a degree of autonomy (such as childcare or services for young people) results in considerable variations over space. Support services for migrant families, both at the level of statutory provision, and in terms of community networks, are much better developed in the larger, more cosmopolitan cities. London, for example, hosts a large number of migrant organizations which provide services (including language tuition) and social support for their members. The influence of location on citizenship entitlement was taken into consideration in designing the sample so as to cover a number of different localities.

In order to deal with these complex spatial dynamics, the children and migration project allowed for an element of policy analysis at each of these levels to contextualize effectively our interpretations of the interviews. At supranational level this involved detailed analysis of Community law and its interpretation by the European Court of Justice (Ackers and Stalford 1999). The importance of understanding the national context within which migrant children were living resulted in the preparation of country reports in each member state by project partners, which summarized both the national legislative and policy context and evidenced examples of unevenness in provision. The various dimensions of context were drawn together in the final analysis and writing-up (see discussion on the roles of partners below).

Culture-boundedness and policy outcomes

Recent years have witnessed increased interest in the promotion and systematic evaluation of policy exchange or 'borrowing', not only within the EU but, also, in guiding policy development in Central European countries. Concerns to ensure that such 'policy borrowing' is both effective and culturally sensitive have emphasized the identification of key socio-cultural, economic and political variables, shaping the evolution of social policy infrastructures. While the importance of placing these infrastructures 'in context' is fundamental to our understanding of the dynamics of policy development, the danger is that the lessons of contextualization will be restricted to an understanding of policy inputs or 'formal policy' (O'Connor 1993, Schunk 1996, Ackers 1998). The more limited attention given to the dynamics of change at the 'recipient end' in comparative research and to the interaction of context with human agency and values restricts the ability of researchers to predict the effectiveness of policy exchange and the impact of policies on citizenship experience. The importance of these structure-agency issues to outcome is well established in single-country studies (Lister 1997) and has informed numerous studies of the mediation of policy by variables of ethnicity and culture within multicultural societies (see, for example, Ahmad 1996 or Robinson 1998).

An important issue emerging from a previous project on gender and migration concerned the ability of women to combine paid work and childrearing, in order to retain the social privileges attached to their status as 'community workers'. Understanding the relationship between women's public and private roles demands consideration not only of the formal policy context, but also of the interface of formal structures with women, as policy recipients, and the implications in terms of outcomes. O'Connor (1993: 509) emphasizes the importance of understanding agency when she says that 'Scandinavian experience points to the fact that policies must be examined not only in terms of formal equality but also in terms of their outcome'. An understanding of Swedish social policy and its impact on gender relations requires an awareness of the political, cultural and economic variables that form the context within which policy has evolved and which has shaped policy inputs. This context is also an important determinant of outcomes in terms of cultural values and attitudes towards labour market participation and social policy interventions. To that extent, culturally-transmitted values may be seen to influence behaviour and policy outcomes: Swedish women may, as a result, articulate a broad acceptance of the legitimacy of combining paid work with childcare, resulting in practice in higher levels of labour market participation. The situation of these women presents complex problems of contextualization as their exposure to a range of culturally-transmitted values, reflecting multiple migrations and, in many cases, mixed nationality partnerships, results in less predictable responses to policy frameworks. This illustrates the problems of conflating the experiences of 'women in Sweden' with those of 'Swedish women in Sweden'.

The children and migration project has raised similar concerns around the identification of relevant cultural boundaries. Country of residence remains an important variable in predicting migrant children's attitudes towards European integration. Indeed, preliminary analysis of the interview findings on children's identity suggests that the children of EU workers in Sweden and the UK (by definition not Swedish or British children) articulate the kind of Euro-sceptic attitudes commonly associated with nationals in the host state (Redmond 1999). Host country is, however, only one dimension of context. The country of emigration, the national background of their parents and grandparents, migration experiences, and so forth, are all important variables in an understanding of attitudes and experiences. The response of children and parents to domestic education policy also needs to be understood in the context not only of host country policy frameworks and cultural values, but also of their pre-migration experiences. This may reflect attitudes towards discipline, the value of different pedagogic approaches, school hours, the relative merits of private or comprehensive education or of international education and denominational schooling (Stalford 1999). The research process thus takes on a 'chromatographic' character, effectively crystallizing out the various dimensions of context and sources of values that shape welfare decisions and citizenship experience. Different national contexts prove to be important variables both in terms of 'sending' and 'receiving' states (bearing in mind also that many families were returnees) and so too are the relevant supranational structures, which not only react to cultural traditions in member states but also generate and transmit values. These examples illustrate the problems of adhering to principles of culture-boundedness, as a key aspect of contextualization, in research concerned with migration. The following section moves on to identify some other methodological challenges for the comparativist interested in researching childhood.

Researching childhood at comparative level

Until the late 1990s, little interest was shown in comparative work on children and childhood. An important exception is Ruxton (1996: 15), who refers to the lack of research 'on legal and policy frameworks, or on the effects of these for children. Neither is there much transnational research comparing outcomes of particular types of service. And children's perceptions of the variety of the circumstances they face have as yet been almost completely ignored'.

The lack of attention to children in comparative policy analysis reflects both the relatively low political priority attached to children's issues and the consequences in terms of data availability. Certainly, in the context of the EU, tightly drawn boundaries of legal competency have lead to an emphasis on 'economic' over 'social' matters. As Pringle (1998: 134) suggests, 'Put simply, children are not workers and are therefore not a primary focus for European Union attention'. To the extent that the EU has extended its influence over key areas of social policy, it has usually done so via skillful interpretation, on the part of the Commission and the European Court of Justice (ECJ), of often tenuous links with what Steiner (1996) calls the 'economic nexus'. The consequences of the low political visibility of children can be seen, not only in the context of children's derived legal entitlement but, also in terms of the availability and quality of secondary data, which generally reflects prevailing political priorities and the emphasis on the Single Market (Levitas and Guy 1996). The most important effect of the lack of legal competence, argues Ruxton (1996: 17), 'is that children receive minimal coverage in EU statistics'.

To the extent that the availability of secondary data has largely driven comparative inquiry, it is not surprising that so little attention has been paid to children. Increasing interest in comparative work has coincided with an explosion in the availability of on-line data facilitated by the growth in, and widespread access to, computing facilities and the Internet. The relative ease and limited cost of using these data 'carries the danger of forgetting that the concepts used in any research derive from the questions and interests of its original intentions.' (Levitas and Guy 1996: 63). The lack of suitable and reliable aggregate data on children and childhood has undoubtedly proved a deterrent to comparative research. It is, however, important not to dismiss entirely the opportunities available and value of secondary analysis. In order to place both Community law and the qualitative work with children in the wider geographical context of intra-Community migration, the children and migration project included cautious analysis of available data on the presence of children in migration stocks and flows, drawn from the European Labour Force Survey and complemented, where possible, by national sources. These statistics provide an important context within which to discuss both policy and qualitative findings.

While issues of data availability and political priority (which directly influence research funding opportunities) partially explain comparativists' relative disinterest in children, there may be other, method-driven explanations for the failure of research undertaken at national level to develop a comparative approach. Recent years have witnessed a mush-rooming of specialist centres, based in UK universities, drawing together and analysing research interest in childhood and child-focused work. The growth in this research area has spawned an interest not only in aspects of policy evaluation and outcomes (or what has become known as 'child-proofing' policies) but also on questions of epistemology and technique. The UN Convention on the Rights of the Child, with its emphasis, in Article 12, on the 'best interests principle' and the 'views of the child' has provided an important impetus both in substantive policy areas (such as child law) and in the context of research practice. Brannen and O'Brien (1996: 1) allude to the relationship between the growing political interest in children's rights and questions of method and approach:

> In the emergent sociology of childhood, children are being conceptually liberated from passive dependency on adults and elevated to the status of social actor. In common with childhood researchers, we have become conscious of the invisibility of children's perspectives and voices and the fact that children's worlds have typically become known through adult accounts.

The notion of 'listening to children' and of actively encouraging the participation of children in research processes has led to a critique of quantitative and other approaches which imply 'an over-reliance on indirect measures of children's well-being and/or adult reports of their adjustment' (Neale and Smart 1998: 10). Concerns about the validity and ethics of using 'proxy' measures (either parents' or teachers' accounts, for example) and the effect of power differentials on the research process, and on the relationship between researchers and child respondents, have encouraged the development of new sources of 'evidence' and a shift in favour of more intensive, qualitative approaches. A Save the Children (1995: 37) report advocates the development of co-researching, or working alongside children in research, 'in order to ensure the outcomes are relevant'. This reflects a commitment to the active participation of children in research processes as a means of generating more sensitive and effective evaluation. Ruxton (1996) suggests that the failure to consider children's perceptions in transnational research may reflect the difficulty and expense implied in attempting to operationalize such approaches at comparative level. No doubt, concerns over the viability and costs of developing qualitative, child-centred, methods in a cross-national context, with serious concerns about language and ethnocentrism, compounded by the 'problem' of diversity in research traditions, has proved a further deterrent to comparative inquiry.

The children and migration project was designed and implemented with these considerations in mind and is presented here, not as a template, but as a means of beginning to identify and discuss approaches to policy evaluation, at comparative level, which are child-centred and relevant to an understanding of migration. It is worth repeating Stanley and Wise's (1993) concerns, at this juncture, about the importance of contextualizing research findings within an open and honest discussion of the 'messiness' of research processes, identifying compromises and 'failures' in order to produce, as far as it is possible, 'unalienated knowledge' and resist the further mystification of research. The dangers of this kind of article lie precisely in the risk of mystification and of conflating wider epistemological concerns with questions of technique, implying that there is something particularly distinctive and specialist about comparative or child-centred methods. Some researchers have questioned the inference that childhood research 'presupposes a special knowledge about children and competence in some particular child-centred techniques [with] the assumption that some techniques are better suited to studying children than others' (Solberg 1996: 58). It is not so much technique that is at issue here but rather broader concerns about the production and interpretation of knowledge. Hantrais and Mangen (1996: 12) make a similar point in the context of comparative inquiry when they suggest that, 'there is nothing particularly distinctive about the methodology of cross-national research'.

The main empirical focus of the children and migration project was on children's perceptions of migration. The project team identified and interviewed parents and children (aged between 11 and 18 years) in 174 families. The interviews were of a qualitative, largely unstructured, nature, and followed a list of topic areas designed to assess the family's migration and family history and its impact on their integration and quality of life. Wherever possible parents and children were interviewed in the language of their preference by the project partners. The interviews were transcribed and translated and sent to England for data analysis. The processes of translation and transcription, required in comparative qualitative research, necessarily moved us further away from children's voices. In practice, the final 'product' reflects the outcome of repeated filtering and interpretation of interviewee's voices by the chain of researchers concerned.

The material was initially 'rough coded' into broad categories and distributed to those team members who expressed an interest in data analysis. Finer coding then took place making use of the MERGE facility which enabled this work to be carried out separately, in different locations before combining it into one 'master' project.

Developing a collaborative approach

The importance of 'situating' research, and in particular, recognizing the influence researchers have, as human agents, on the generation and interpretation of knowledge is common to all research. These broader ontological and epistemological considerations affect all forms of social research, irrespective of substantive or spatial scope. Recognition of researchers' cultural backgrounds as key components of contextualization is, however, of particular significance to comparative inquiry. The requirement to have partners in EU-funded projects has encouraged a move away from 'safari' approaches in favour of more collaborative working. The level and quality of research collaboration at the different phases in the life of comparative projects, nevertheless, varies considerably. Arguably pressures to develop very large research teams may actually militate against effective collaboration since such teams become unwieldy, imply hierarchy and administrative overload. The sheer costs of team meetings in these projects typically results in one or more partners assuming responsibility for initial project definition (and submission), research design, analysis and report-writing, whilst the majority of partners perform a 'data gathering' function, leaving very little scope for contextualization. Effective contextualization, in terms of recognition of the influence of culture throughout the research process, demands more genuine and participatory involvement of partners from project design and identification of issues and approaches (perhaps the most crucial stage) through to implementation and interpretation of findings. The extent to which this is achievable depends on the financial resources available and the commitments of partners.

The children and migration project involved on-going collaboration between the partners and participants in the UK and abroad. This commenced at the project design and proposal phase and was facilitated via team meetings, which alternated between member states, and visits during the course of the research. The alternation of meeting locations between partner countries together with the visits underlines the importance of spending time in partner countries, in order to build up insight and experience of the research contexts. In this respect also, the issue of context is quite different from that in other forms of research, as the concerns to 'match' researchers with interviewees, in terms of national background, becomes problematic. By definition the respondents are not nationals. The importance of partners derives from their awareness of domestic policy frameworks, of the values underpinning them and of the migration histories and the spatial location of different groups. In some cases, it was interesting to compare the response of interviewees to interviewers from different backgrounds. This was seen particularly strongly in the attempts of Portuguese researchers to access migrant children in international schools. Numerous attempts to set up interviews with representatives of some of these schools failed. When the British researchers arrived in Portugal, as representatives of a British university, appointments were made immediately. In other cases, Portuguese researchers received little or no response to repeated attempts to contact key informants in the migrant community.

When approached by the UK researchers, however, they were immediately responsive, providing a list of contacts.

The meetings involved the presentation of papers building on partners' specific expertise. The British group provided material on Community law, the Greek partner on intercultural social work, and the Portuguese team on comparative work with children. The meetings were used to 'thrash out' issues of method and approach. This often proved difficult given the diversity of disciplinary and cultural backgrounds, but was stimulating and effective in achieving 'compromises'. In the context of working collaboratively with a team of partners from a range of cultural and disciplinary backgrounds, however, compromise does not necessarily imply sloppiness or a lack of rigour but rather, the benefits of negotiation and shared experience that researchers are able to avoid in single-country studies. Materials and transcripts of interviews and reports were circulated on an on-going basis, and the project director distributed regular 'project updates' by e-mail summarizing decisions and debates with individual partners, who produced both interim and final reports on aspects of sampling, domestic policy and national migration traditions in order to promote the effective contextualization of the interview material.

Constraints on project finance and partners' time have made it difficult to involve all participants in data analysis. Where possible, partners were invited to come to England to receive training in the use of NUD*IST and to collaborate in this part of the project. Where this was not possible, partners were invited to identify areas of interest to them and contribute sections to the final report and publications based on the research. They were provided with partially analysed data or information on other aspects of the research not dependent upon the interview findings. Drafts of papers were circulated to partners for comments prior to their inclusion in any reports. In practice, much of the final report was drafted in England by the co-ordinating team. The experience of co-ordinating these projects suggests that effective collaboration in final report-writing is both time-consuming and difficult, particularly working in a second language. Furthermore, it is rarely possible to achieve a level of funding which allows for salary recovery for this phase of the work.

Conclusions

This paper has presented the method used in a comparative project concerned to evaluate the status and experiences of a group of children who have moved between member states. It has discussed the relevance and applicability of concepts of context and culture-boundedness and the challenges faced by researchers embarking on cross-national studies of childhood. The discussion around contextualization emphasizes the importance of context not only to our understanding of policy evolution but also to outcome (and the interface of structures with users). Research involving 'mobile' citizens presents particular problems concerning the choice of relevant contexts. Whilst this forms an explicit focus of the research in question, it is perhaps important for other areas of research to recognize the 'fluidity' and wider cultural mixes present within national contexts and their impact on values and outcomes. A particular concern of the project was the development of an approach capable of 'listening to children'. Without doubt, the complexities of language, involving not only transcription but also translation and team-working introduce a wider range of 'filters' than smaller, single-person, single-country projects. In that sense, we are hearing not children's voices as such, but rather their interpretation and re-interpretation in the course of the research process. This represents a good example of 'compromise in method', involving to some extent the sacrifice of quality. The benefits of the quantity and diversity of this sample, however, and our ability to address a wider range of experiences arguably outweigh the disadvantages. Moreover, our ability to evaluate aspects of supranational policy from user's perspectives, is clearly a distinctive feature of this approach. Whilst the supranational focus represents a particular feature of the research, it may, in practice, become increasingly difficult not to deal with the interface of supranational and national policy as member states influence policy development and the tentacles of Community law and policy permeate domestic social policy.

References

Ackers, H.L. and Abbott, P. (1996) *Social Policy for Nurses and the Caring Professions* (Buckingham: Open University Press).

Ackers, H.L. (1998) *Shifting Spaces. Women, Citizenship and Migration within the European Union* (Bristol: Policy Press).

Ackers, H.L. and Stalford, H.E. (1999) Children, migration and family policy in the European Union: intra-community mobility and the status of children in EC law. *Children and Youth Services Review*, **21**(8–9), 699–721.

Ahmad, W.I.U. and Atkin, K. (eds) (1996) *'Race' and Community Care* (Buckingham: Open University Press).

Boyle, P., Halfacree, K. and Robinson, V. (1998) *Exploring Contemporary Migration* (Harlow: Longman).

Brannen, J. and O'Brien, M. (1996) *Children in Families* (London: Falmer Press).

Hantrais, L. and Mangen, S. (1996) *Cross-National Research Methods in the Social Sciences* (London: Pinter).

Kelson, G.A. and DeLaet, D.L. (1999) *Gender and Immigration* (London: Macmillan).

Levitas, R. and Guy, W. (1996) *Interpreting Official Statistics* (London: Routledge).

Lister, R. (1997) *Citizenship: Feminist Perspectives* (London: Macmillan).

Neale, B. and Smart, C. (1998) Agents or dependants? Struggling to listen to children in family law and family research, *Centre for Research on Family, Kinship and Childhood Working Paper* No. 3.

O'Connor, J. S. (1993) Gender class and citizenship in the comparative analysis of welfare states; theoretical and methodological issues, *The British Journal of Sociology*, **44**(3), 501–519.

Pringle, K. (1998) *Children and Social Welfare in Europe* (Buckingham: Open University Press).

Redmond, M. (1999) Children, young people and identity formations within the European Union, Paper to the Socio-Legal Studies Association Conference, Loughborough University.

Robinson, L. (1998) *'Race', Communication and the Caring Professions* (Buckingham: Open University Press).

Ruxton, S. (1996) *Children in Europe* (London: NCH Action for Children).

Save the Children (1995) *Towards a Children's Agenda* (London: Save the Children).

Schunk, M. (1996) Constructing models of the welfare mix: care options of frail elders. In L. Hantrais and S. Mangen (eds) *Cross-National Research Methods in the Social Sciences* (London: Pinter), pp 84–94.

Solberg, A. (1996) The challenge in child research: from 'being' to 'doing'. In J. Brannen and M. O'Brien (eds) *Children in Families* (London: Falmer Press), pp 53–66.

Spicker, P. (1991) The principle of subsidiarity and the social policy of the European Community. *Journal of European Social Policy*, **1** (3), 53–66.

Stalford, H. E. (1999) The educational status and experience of the children of EU migrant workers. *Children, Citizenship and Internal Migration in the EU*. Final Report to the European Commission, DGXXII, November.

Stanley, L. and Wise, S. (1993) *Breaking Out Again. Feminist Ontology and Epistemology* (London: Routledge).

Steiner, J. (1996) *Textbook on EC Law* (London: Blackstone Press).

INDEX